Teaching The
ATTRACTION PRINCIPLE™
to Children

Practical Strategies for Parents and
Teachers to Help Children
Manifest a Better World

Thomas Haller and
Chick Moorman

Personal Power Press
Merrill, Michigan

Teaching The ATTRACTION PRINCIPLE™ to Children

Practical Strategies for Parents and Teachers to Help Children Manifest a Better World

Copyright 2008 by Thomas Haller, Chick Moorman, and Personal Power Press

Library of Congress Catalogue Card Number: 2007939935

ISBN 978-0-9772321-6-1

Printed in the United States of America

Personal Power Press
P.O. Box 547, Merrill, MI 48637

Cover Design
Zachary Parker/kadak graphics
kdp431@gmail.com

Book Design
Connie Thompson/Graphics etcetera:
connie2@lighthouse.net

TABLE OF CONTENTS

Foreword vii

Introduction xi

Section One 1

The Gravity Principle 2

The Magnetism Principle 3

Gravity, Magnetism and Our Lives 3

The Attraction Principle 4

Vibrations 5

Thoughts 5

The Self-Fulfilling Prophecy .6

Plant to Harvest 7

Attention 8

Buffer Zone 8

Seeing What Is 9

Beyond What Is 11

Reframing 12

Solution Seeking 14

Taking Control 14

Focusing on Lack 15

Look for Evidence 17

Emotional Feedback 18

The Distraction Principle 20

Conscious Creation 20

Contrast 22

Using Contrast 24

Revisiting Wants 25

Allowing 27

Allowing Statements 28

Positive Picturing 30

Affirmations 32

Act As If 34

Purposeful Anticipation 36

Use Surprise 37

Giving 38

Action 39

Move Up Before You Move In 40

Gratitude 45

Keep It a Secret 48

Allowing Revisited 48

Section Two 51

Your Role 52

The Attraction Principle .57

Vibrations 59

Thoughts 61

The Self-Fulfilling Prophecy 64

Plant to Harvest 67

Attention 71

Buffer Zone 76

What Is and Beyond 78

Reframing 84

Solution Seeking 86

Taking Control 89

Focusing on Lack 97

Look for Evidence 100

Emotional Feedback 101

The Distraction Principle 104

Conscious Creation 108

Using Contrast 120

Revisiting Wants 123

Allowing 125

Allowing Statements 128

Positive Picturing 134

Affirmations 138

Act As If 142

Purposeful Anticipation 149

Action 152

Gratitude 154

Conclusion 157

About the Authors 163

Bibliography 171

Our Vision: Healing Acres 179

Other Books and Products 181

FOREWORD

by Jack Canfield

A friend commented to me the other day that I have been part of the two biggest phenomena in the furthering of the human potential movement in the past twenty years - the creation of the *Chicken Soup for the Soul* series and the release of the blockbuster movie and the publication of the bestselling book *The Secret*. Well, I do indeed feel blessed to have been a central part of those two projects, which have allowed me to contribute to the lives of tens of millions of people around the world and have led to an incredible journey and life for me and my family. One of the most fulfilling and fun parts of that journey has been travelling all over the world teaching seminars and speaking at "Secret Conferences" with many of the other teachers from The Secret.

As we speak at these conferences, all of us (Lisa Nichols, Bob Proctor, John Assaraf, Reverend Michael Beckwith, John Gray, James Ray, Lee Brower, Marie Diamond, Marci Shimoff, Hale Dwoskin and the others) are always approached afterwards by people asking us what's the best way to teach children about The Secret - the law of attraction and how it works. Up until now we have only been able to say, "Show them the movie and ask them to talk about how they think they could apply the basic ideas to their life. Have them set some goals, create a vision board, visualize and use affirmations." Most of the people had already done that. They wanted more. They wanted a set of simple principles, effective practices and easy-to-use strategies they could apply on a daily basis. Well, finally, with the publication of this book, they (and you) have the answer to the question. And what a wonderful book it is!

I have known Chick Moorman for almost thirty years. He has been writing books and conducting workshops for parents and teachers longer than anyone I know in the human potential movement. He has a dedication to parents, teachers and children that is unsurpassed. I have only known Thomas Haller for a few years, but his dedication and commitment to making a difference are equal to Chick's. I am thrilled that they have taken the time to develop and test out these ideas with parents and teachers all across the country, teach them in their seminars and workshops, and now present them in this book.

This book will teach you how to both intentionally and spontaneously apply these strategies with children of all ages - preschool to high school - both at home and in the classroom. You will learn how to teach and how to facilitate the application of the basic principles of living an intentional, purpose-filled life, creating the results you want, and ultimately contributing to a world that works for everyone. Chick and Thomas have made these ideas simple to under-stand and easy to apply. There are tons of great ideas that you can begin to use immediately. I still have two sixteen-year-old boys and a thirteen-year-old girl liv-ing at home, and after one quick read through the book, I found myself applying some of the ideas and techniques with my own children - and I teach this stuff every day! Like me, I know that you will find a lot of practical wisdom between the covers of this book.

I send you my love and my best wishes for success-fully applying the principles and techniques and cre-ating a life filled with love, joy, and all of your dreams come true for yourself and your children.

Jack Canfield

Co-author of *Chicken Soup for the Parent's Soul* and *Chicken Soup for the Teacher's Soul;* Author of *Effortless Success* and *Jack Canfield's Keys to Living the Law of Attraction;* Featured Teacher in *The Secret*

INTRODUCTION

Do you know "the Secret"? Have you heard it talked about? Has anyone offered to share it with you? Have you been invited to a special viewing of *The Secret* DVD or a reading of the book by Rhonda Byrne? If not, you are missing out on something millions of people all over the world have been talking about and putting into practice in their lives over the past few years.

People wishing to create wealth, find a new job, or connect with their soul mate are learning how to make the Secret as popularized by Byrne's book and the DVD work for them. So are people who want health, a new home, a satisfying marriage, or a more intimate relationship with God. New materials purporting to offer the secret to business success, joy, harmony, and abundance are being created every day. You will find a sampling of these books in the bibliography of this volume.

To underscore the popularity of the Secret, debunkers have risen to the bait and are now publishing anti-Secret books and related materials. These criticisms are currently appearing in bookstores as well as on the Internet.

New material on the Secret and the principle upon which it is based, the Law of Attraction, appears regularly. Yet something seems to be missing. There is a noticeable hole in the current collection of information: how to teach what we refer to as "the Attraction Principle" to children. We have noticed that void and intend to fill it with this book.

As parenting experts we are frequently asked about how to use the Attraction Principle with children. Parents and professional educators want to know. Can the Secret and related concepts be applied to everyday parenting? Can teachers use the Attraction Principle in their classrooms? Can it be used to create responsible, caring, confident children? The answer to all of these questions is "yes." This book will show you how.

Indeed, all parents and educators are presently using the Attraction Principle with children whether they know it or not. Some are using it consciously, with intentionality. Others remain unconscious of how they are implementing it in their lives. Both groups are using it, nonetheless.

Some parents and educators are using the Attraction Principle and related concepts to attract helpless, unempowered, unmotivated characteristics in their children. Others are using it to attract responsible, caring, confident characteristics. Some are using it to produce stress, conflict, and drama in their parenting or teaching lives. Others are using the concepts to generate peace, harmony, and family or classroom unity.

Our goal in writing *Teaching The ATTRACTION PRIN-CIPLE™ to Children* is to show you what happens when this important principle meets real-life parenting or teaching situations. We want to help you see how the same strategies that you can use to build wealth or health can also be used to effectively manifest your heart's desire in your family or classroom.

The book is divided into two main sections. The first briefly describes the Attraction Principle, defines it, and explains the conscious creating process. It is not our intent to recreate what has already been written in the many books that eloquently detail the concepts revealed in *The Secret*. Instead, we will focus on how to best use these concepts to create the family and classroom life you fervently desire.

Section One is designed to increase your understanding of the Attraction Principle as the first step in learning to use it with the important children in your life. Becoming conscious of how this critical concept is operating in your life is necessary for you to take control of it and use it with intentionality to create the parenting or teaching life you desire. Your heightened awareness will be your pathway to the place where you will purposefully use these important ideas with your children or students.

The importance of thoughts, beliefs, emotions and expectations is covered in Section One. Here we demonstrate the role your emotions play in the process of creating the family or classroom life you always wanted. You will learn to use your emotions as a personal feedback system to generate the data necessary to maintain or make changes in the thoughts, images and beliefs that are creating your present parenting or classroom reality.

Section One will also show you how to harness and use the power of intention. You will learn how to create strong, specific desires and deliberately set them forth in a consistent manner. You will learn to make your intentions conscious and purposeful in order to positively affect your behavior as you move forward, creating the classroom or family that you intend. In this section you will learn to examine whether on not you are blocking your desires from coming to you. You will learn how to use the process of allowing by eliminating doubt and worry.

Section Two focuses exclusively on practical strategies to help you teach your children to use the Attraction Principle in their own lives. This knowledge and application will help them become the creators of their own reality and decrease the chance that they will see themselves as victims.

Tots to teens can learn the concepts inherent in the Attraction Principle if modeled and taught by adults who consistently employ a process of mutual respect. In this section you will learn to become a soul model for children, nourishing their spirit as you guide them down their own path of unfolding and creating who and what they intend to be.

The book you now hold in your hands is here because you attracted it into your life. It could not have come to you without your permission. You helped us write it by your desire to have it. You wanted to understand these concepts and learn these skills. We felt it and we responded.

So now you have it, *Teaching The ATTRACTION PRINCIPLE™ to Children*. It is our firm and heartfelt expectation that you will use the material in this book to create the family or classroom you always wanted. We anticipate you will use it to become the parent or teacher you always wanted to be. We expect you will use it to bring forth the power, clarity, and results that help you touch the souls of the important children in your lives.

We sincerely appreciate your attention to this book. Thank you for wanting it. Thank you for finding it. And thank you for using it.

We are continuing to enjoy the process.

Thomas Haller and Chick Moorman

SECTION ONE

This book is about teaching the Attraction Principle to children. To do that well, it is necessary to learn to use this important principle in your own life.

It is difficult to teach children to read if you don't love reading, if you don't do it regularly in your own life, if you don't experience its value.

It is difficult to teach children to swim if you don't love swimming, if you don't do it regularly in your own life, if you don't experience its value.

Section One is designed to help you love the Attraction Principle, use it regularly in your own life, and experience its value. Only then will you be ready to teach its important lessons to children.

The Attraction Principle is not complicated. Nor is it long or drawn out. It is simply this: *We create our own reality by attracting into our lives what we give our attention, thoughts, emotion, energy and focus to.* This concept works regardless of whether our attention, thoughts, emotion, energy or focus is positive or negative.

Authors, philosophers, politicians, and others have been writing and talking about the Attraction Principle for ages. In 1906, William Atkinson wrote *Thought Vibration or The Law of Attraction in Thought*. *The Science of Getting Rich* was published in 1910 by Wallace Wattles. Norman Vincent Peale wrote *The Power of Positive Thinking* in 1952. You will find more detail in the bibliography concerning the large number of authors and famous people who have written and/or spoken about the Attraction Principle.

So the Attraction Principle is hardly a secret. In fact, it is only a secret if you are not aware of it.

The Gravity Principle

If you drop the book you are holding right now, what will happen to it? It will fall to the ground.

The book responds to the Gravity Principle. We expect it. We believe in it. We have even come to depend on it.

When we throw something into the air, we know it is coming back down. We watch our step on a ladder because we are certain that a false step is not going to send us higher.

No one questions the existence of gravity. We accept it because we are provided with constant visual proof of its existence. Moment to moment we see and feel the results of gravity.

The Magnetism Principle

Magnetism is another well-known principle. It is the principle that holds galaxies together. It is the central force that operates in our universe. In fact, the planet Earth is a giant magnet.

In classrooms throughout the world, school children learn about the invisible field that surrounds magnets. That magnetic field attracts like objects. Any child who has ever played with a magnet has witnessed the effect of a paper clip or other small metal object literally jumping in the direction of the magnet until the two are connected.

The scientific explanation of this phenomenon is simple. The atoms in a magnet are lined up and vibrating in a perfect north/south alignment. When the magnet enters the field of a piece of metal, the atoms in the metal begin to line up to match the north/south alignment of the magnet. The greater the alignment of the atoms becomes, the more the metal is attracted to the magnet and the more like a magnet it behaves.

Gravity, Magnetism, and Our Lives

The young child who has no words to explain the Gravity Principle understands it soon enough. He drops a rattle or a spoon, falls as he attempts to walk, or spills milk. Although he has no name for it, the effects of gravity quickly become evident.

Gravity works in our lives whether we know its name, use it intentionally, or not. No one can ignore the Gravity Principle for very long without coming face-to-face with dramatic results.

Like a magnet, our minds become magnetized with the dominating thoughts and emotions we hold there. Those thoughts and emotions send out vibrations into the universe and attract the essence of what we are thinking and feeling.

Like the Gravity Principle, this attraction process occurs whether you have a name for it or not. It happens whether you do it intentionally or not. It is currently at work in your life whether you believe it or not. And it is affecting your children or students.

The Attraction Principle

What we think about the most we attract into our lives. This powerful force, the Attraction Principle, like gravity and magnetism, is unseen. Yet its results are visible and presently surround us. This force is currently at work drawing to each of us the results of our dominating thoughts.

Did you ever notice that the person who thinks and talks the most about illness is the one who has the most illness? The one who talks about lack of abundance is the person who never seems to have enough money. The parent who talks about and thinks about the rebellion of his teenager gets the most rebellion. The teacher who thinks predominately about the disinterest of her students attracts a class of disinterested students. The man who complains bitterly and often about his ex-wife attracts an increasing amount of conflict and incidence of negative situations to fuel his need to complain about her.

We all behave like a magnet, constantly attracting the core of what we are thinking and feeling.

Vibrations

Only two kinds of vibrations exist in our lives, positive and negative. Every thought you think, every image you hold, every emotion you feel or mood you hang onto sends out a positive or negative vibration.

When you think your student is lazy, you are sending out a vibration. When your thoughts focus on the increasing size of your daughter's waistline, you are transmitting a vibration. Likewise, when your focus is on your child's smile, his kind heart, or his persistence, you are sending a vibration.

Thoughts

Our thoughts send vibrations into the universe, and through the magnetic power of the principle, the essence of what we think about is attracted to us. Essentially, we get what we habitually think about. This occurs whether what we are thinking about is something we desire or something we definitely do not prefer.

If you think about your child's bullying, talk about it,

or worry about it, you are attracting more of that into her life and into your present reality.

If you think and talk about the effort your soccer players put into practice and the games, you attract more of the same to your team and to your life experience.

If you talk about your child being a troublemaker, you attract troublemaking. If you think thoughts of your child as a leader, you attract leadership.

The Self-Fulfilling Prophecy

The Attraction Principle fits perfectly with the self-fulfilling prophecy. If you think of your child as cooperative and talk about it frequently, you are more likely to see her as cooperative. If you see her as cooperative, you are more likely to develop the belief that she is, indeed, cooperative. When you believe she is cooperative, you are more likely to notice times when she chooses a behavior that could be interpreted as cooperative.

As you notice more incidences where she appears cooperative to you, you confirm your beliefs that she is cooperative. Since you now have proof, you see her as even more cooperative and think and talk more about her as if she was cooperative. In time, the child begins to see herself as cooperative.

Congratulations. Your prophecy has just come true. Finally, you have created the child as cooperative.

This process operates the same whether you think of a

child as aggressive, loving, lazy, disorganized, manipulative, friendly, studious, or respectful.

What you think about increases. The more you choose to focus on the positive or negative, the more power you bring to it. The longer you persist in focusing on it, the stronger you make it in your reality.

Plant to Harvest

Parents, teachers, coaches, childcare workers, and others who work with children, take note. Your thoughts are like planting seeds. What kind of harvest are you interested in? If you want apples, we suggest you plant apple seeds. Planting orange seeds will not produce apple trees.

Carrot seeds fail to turn into lettuce, no matter how often you water them. Likewise, positive outcomes are not produced by thinking negative thoughts. Teachers, how do you want to grow your students? Do you want them to be confident, cooperative, respectful, responsible, and caring? Do you want them to develop a zest for learning? Are the seeds (thoughts) you are planting today going to produce the crop you desire?

Parents, what seeds are you sowing with your children? Are they going to bloom to become trustworthy, self-reliant, decisionally literate, persistent, and charitable?

Remember, the thoughts you place in your mind will attract like behaviors.

Attention

What you give your attention to increases. What do you see, think about, and talk about in regard to your children or students? Whatever it is, you can be sure of one thing: It will increase.

Do you see a troubled youth or someone who is searching for her own path? Do you see a frustrating problem or an opportunity to help the child learn an important lesson? Do you think about the inconvenience a sick child causes you or the chance to be comforting and supportive while he is ill?

When a student spills paint, do you see it as awful or as an opportunity to teach the entire class about cleanup procedures? Where do you direct your attention? Where would you put it if you remembered that what you give your attention to increases?

We are each responsible for what we see and for the amount of attention we give that choice of perception.

Buffer Zone

There is a time lapse between when you begin to think about something and when it shows up in your life. This buffer zone allows you the opportunity to notice your thoughts and redirect them to the things you want to purposefully manifest in your parenting or teaching life.

So if you hear yourself talking negatively or catch yourself thinking negatively, the thought will not immediately appear in physical form. You have time to change your thoughts.

If you catch yourself thinking of your child's bedwetting, stop. Redirect your thoughts. Think about the positive aspect of the bedwetting, even if it is only a small part of the whole situation. Remember how your child takes responsibility for putting his wet sheets in the washer or changes his own bed each day when he gets home from school. Think about that instead and you'll be sending positive vibrations into the universe.

If you continue to give your attention to a situation - whether it is something you want or something you do not want - it will increasingly enter your experience. When you catch yourself thinking of the D your child got on her report card, switch your thoughts. Dwell on the two Bs that were also on the report card. Or focus on the comment her third-hour teacher wrote: "Manda is improving steadily."

You can think about the thumb sucking or about your child's use of the teething ring that he occasionally puts in his mouth. You can focus on the thought that your child only has two friends or be grateful that he has two great buddies. How you perceive these situations and think about them is up to you.

Seeing *What Is*

"You're not grounded in reality," a teacher complained at one of our full-day staff development seminars. "By thinking only of what I want, I am ignoring *what is.* I have to deal with *what is*, and I have to do it now!"

We are not suggesting you ignore *what is. What is* has to be dealt with on a physical level. If a student is flunking your algebra class, a plan needs to be created and implemented to respond appropriately to that situation. If your students are failing to turn in assignments on time, action is needed.

Parents, if your oldest son is hitting his younger brother, more is called for than simply thinking positive thoughts. If he dips his sleeve in catsup and touches his sleeve to his pants, a physical response from you is appropriate before the mess spreads any further.

In each of the situations above, action is necessary. And the quality of the action you take in each instance will be largely determined by the decision you make about where to place your focus. You can control the mental focus of your thought and/or the emotion even as you work to change the situation on a physical level.

As you take action, will your predominant thoughts be on the algebra grade you desire or on the one that currently exists? Will your focus and attention be on late papers or on the ones you expect to be on time in the future?

Will your parental attention concentrate on the current hitting or on touching each other gently next time? Will your energy be directed at unsightly manners or at teaching how to keep sleeves clean during dinner?

If you continue to focus on what is, you increase your chances of staying stuck in the rut of *what is*. Putting your attention, energy, and emotion there will anchor you in place. You will remain stuck in the *what is* you are currently seeing.

Beyond *What Is*

Because of the extraordinary amount of attention we give to *what is*, not much changes for many of us. If change is what you desire, focus on what you desire instead of on *what is*.

A mother we know tells us regularly what a bully her ten-year-old son is. Each time she talks with us she recites the incriminating incidents with strong emotion and fine detail, as if she needed to prove her case to doubting jurors. She repeats stories from the past and embellishes them slightly each time. Most harmful of all, she relates these incidents to us with her son present so that he hears her interpretations and is reminded continually of what a bully he is.

What this mother is doing is using a magnifying glass to focus on one aspect of her son's experience. This special magnifying glass helps her get really close to each bullying incident, examine it in detail, and blow it up in her consciousness so it becomes larger than it is in reality. She apparently didn't read the warning on the lens that says, "Images you magnify appear larger than they actually are." Her thoughts, energy, emotion, and attention are making the bullying behavior of her son larger than it actually is. This simultaneously shrinks the size of his positive actions and traits in both her eyes and in his.

A helpful response here would be to look at the situation, define the problem, and begin a search for solutions. By searching for solutions you give attention to how you prefer things to be rather than to *what is.*

Whether you are this child's parent or teacher, it is helpful to see the result you want as already completed. If you are presently unable to see him five years from now having transformed bullying to assertiveness, then do this: See him as *on the way* to arriving there. Your job is to help him get there. Defining him as a bully isn't going to do that.

Reframing

Another way to alter how you see *what is* is to reframe it. This technique is a lot like reframing a picture. Perhaps you have owned a picture that didn't look quite the way you wanted it to look. You put another frame around it and it still didn't look exactly right. Then you tried a third frame and the picture immediately took on a whole new look and feel. It seemed like a new picture. You loved it.

This same concept can be applied to how you see your student or child. We know a woman whose teachers wrote on almost every report card a version of, "She talks too much." "Fancy needs to cut down on her talking," "Her constant talking is distracting," and "Fancy's talking gets her in a lot of trouble" were specific comments she received as a student. The "talks too much" theme was echoed by elementary, middle school, and high school teachers alike. Apparently, concentrating on the *what is* didn't change her desire to talk out in class much.

Fancy's own mother thought she talked too much as well and often made derogatory and shaming comments to her about it. "Why can't you ever stop talking?" and "Who do you think wants to hear your opinion, anyway?" she would challenge her daughter.

Today, Fancy is a professional speaker and makes an abundant living traveling all over the world . . . talking. When you put the professional-speaker frame around talking, that behavior takes on a whole new look and feel. Talking becomes a good thing, a positive attribute.

At a parent/teacher conference recently, the mother complained that her six-year-old was "stubborn." "Good," the teacher responded. Taken aback, the parent inquired, "What do you mean 'good'? I just told you he was stubborn." "That's good," said the teacher, "because no one will be able to push him around or move him with peer pressure." Because of the reframing of "stubborn" by this skilled teacher, the mother was able to look at her child's behavior with new eyes.

An "anger explosion" can be looked on differently when it becomes "sharing your feelings." "Tattling" can be reframed as "positive reporting." Don't we all wish someone had done some positive reporting before each of the recent school shootings?

Do you like the *what is* you currently see? If not, move your attention away from it. Move it to what could be, to the classroom or family life you desire. One helpful way to move away from *what is* to switch your focus from what is to the search for solutions.

Solution Seeking

When you face your next parenting challenge, examine where you invest your time, energy, and attention. Do you concentrate on fixing blame or on fixing the problem? Does your focus move ahead in the direction of looking for possibilities, or does it stay stuck on *what is?*

If you send energy to the solution, you are sending energy toward what you want. If you send energy to the problem, you are directing energy to what you don't want.

Next time you experience yourself caught in a parenting or teaching dilemma, focus on the *what is* of the problem and notice how you feel. What thoughts are you thinking? What feelings do those thoughts create? Our prediction is that the feelings you experience will be negative. And those feelings were generated by the thoughts you had been thinking, mostly negative.

Then begin the search for a solution focusing on what *could be* and again monitor your thoughts. Notice how you are feeling now. Our hunch is that the feeling this time will be positive, produced by the positive thoughts you had been thinking.

Taking Control

You can take control of your own parenting or teaching life by understanding the Attraction Principle and directing your attention to what you want to create.

What you think about increases. The longer you focus on it, the more it increases. The more strength you give it, the more evidence of its existence shows up in your life. The more evidence you see, the stronger your belief becomes. The stronger your belief, the more you think about it.

You are in charge of where you direct your attention. How often you put your attention there and the intensity with which you do it is also under your control. By taking conscious control you can attract desired experiences into your parenting or teaching life and you can release those experiences that you don't want.

Focusing on Lack

Often we fail to attract what we want in our parenting or teaching situations because we focus on the lack of it. When we think about what we want and then let our thoughts go to the fact that we don't have it yet, we are preventing it from coming to us. We are hindering ourselves.

Thinking about your student's aggressiveness pushes away his assertiveness. Dwelling on your child's dishonesty repels her truthfulness. Giving attention to her disorganization keeps her organization from appearing to you.

Another way we focus on lack and attract it to us is by using negative words. Perhaps you have heard yourself make some of the following comments to your children or students.

"Don't run."
"Stop whining."
"No yelling in here."
"Hitting your sister is *not* appropriate."
"He *never* comes home on time."
"Don't you talk to me like that."
"Don't forget."
"End that anger right now."
"There is *no* rush."
"Talking with your mouth full is *not* helpful."

The words you use are important. Words send out vibrations. Be aware that the universe, your children, and your students do not hear "no" or "don't."

If I tell you, "Don't think of a purple giraffe," your thought goes immediately to a purple giraffe. The picture you create in your head is one of a purple giraffe.

The subconscious mind does not hear the words "no," "don't," "not," and "stop." Similar words do not register in our own or in our children's biocomputer (brain).

When you say, "Don't run," to your child, the word that registers in her consciousness is RUN. The picture that is created in her mind is one of RUNNING.

Use precise words to create positive vibrations in your child's consciousness. "Please walk" plants the positive thought and creates the positive picture you want in your daughter's biocomputer. "Next time, use your words to tell your sister you are angry," sends your son the positive vibration as well as teaches the behavior you want in the future.

Other examples of positive Parent Talk and Teacher Talk include:

"Please use your indoor voice."
"I will understand you better when you finish chewing before you start talking."
"Remember to . . ."
"He was on time twice this week."
"You have time to get ready in a relaxed manner."

Look for Evidence

Look at what you are experiencing and you will see evidence of what you have been thinking. There is nothing that simply shows up in your life uninvited. You attract all of it.

Use what you see as feedback. Do you notice a frustrating parenting life? Or do you see loving, connected family times? What you see is evidence of what you have been previously thinking.

Teachers, do you see conflict and student resistance? Or do you see a challenging opportunity? What you see will give you important clues to what you have been thinking.

When you look around, do you like what you notice? Do you see responsibility or lack of it? Do you see empathy or its absence? Do you see procrastination or getting started quickly?

If you don't like what you see, it is time to change your vibrations. It is time to alter your thoughts and your emotions.

Emotional Feedback

Looking for evidence in your thoughts by attempting to monitor them throughout the day would be a full-time activity. An alternative to the time-consuming task of noticing every thought is to pay attention to how you are feeling.

Your emotions send a physical signal that indicates whether or not you are creating what you want.

To be an effective parent or educator it's important to pay attention to your feelings and listen to them. Become conscious of the messages your feelings are sending you. Once you notice your emotion, you are at power. You can now make a conscious decision about what to do or what to think using the data you received. When you feel frustrated, annoyed, irritated, or angry, you can easily recognize the discord and move your thoughts to something different.

When irritation surfaces after you spot your three-year-old using permanent markers on your kitchen wall, you can think how age appropriate it is for three-year-olds to do that and what a perfect time this is to teach her about where to engage in artistic exploration.

When you feel frustration registering in your stomach after noticing wet towels on the bathroom floor, you can think about the time your teen did all the laundry herself without being asked.

When your fifth-grader argues with you about inter-pretation of a classroom rule and your stomach begins to send you signals of annoyance, you can picture this student in the future standing up for his rights as a responsible adult.

This is not to mean that you ignore the *what is* of the present situation and sit idly by, being content with simply changing your thoughts. Yes, action may be required in each instance. Take the action you deem appropriate, and if you delay that action until you have managed your mind by choosing the thought you want, you will insure that the action you do take flows from a place of higher consciousness within you.

Your emotions will let you know if your thoughts are in vibration with what you want. Negative emotion will occur if your thoughts are moving you in the direction of what you don't want.

The process of using your emotions to guide you is stated below.

1. Notice your feelings. Pay attention to them.
2. Move closer to those things that feel good.
3. Move away from things that feel bad.
4. Rearrange your thoughts until you feel good.

When you are feeling positive emotion, you can be confident that you are attracting what you want.

The Distraction Principle

Sometimes you might feel yourself caught in a negative snarl. You notice negative feelings, begin to pay attention to them, and even create some thoughts that move you closer to those things that feel good. Yet you still feel trapped in a negative mood.

You think one new thought that moves you slightly closer to where you want to be, then another, and another. Still the negativity clings to you like Velcro. What now?

Now is the time to activate the Distraction Principle. Do or think something totally different. Take a time-out. Read a book. Listen to music. Stop at a garage sale. Mow the grass. Play with your dog. Ride a horse. Put totally different data in your mind. Or do a mindless activity like cleaning your horse stall or chopping wood. Purposefully distract yourself until you can feel the energy shift.

When the Distraction Principle has done its job, you can return to purposefully creating the teaching or parenting life you desire. It is important that you return to purposefully creating. If you don't, the Distraction Principle becomes the Avoidance Principle.

Conscious Creation

The process of conscious creation in your classroom or home begins with identifying your wants. It continues when you place focused attention and energy on those wants and it ends when you allow your wants into your experience. The steps to conscious creation are:

1. Identify a want.

2. Focus your attention and energy on that want.

3. Allow the want into your experience.

Most parents and teachers spend little time figuring out what they want. Often they appear to be too busy observing and dealing with *what is*. One parent told us recently at one of our workshops, "I don't want to hear back talk from my son anymore." "So, talking back is what you don't want. If that is what you don't want, what is it that you do want?" we asked him. "I don't know and I don't care," the father replied. "I just want him to stop talking back."

The point to remember here is that the conscious creation process continues to operate whether you are thinking about what you want or what you don't want. If you are thinking you don't want your child coming home late or your students cheating on tests, you are consciously creating just as much as you are when your attention is on your desire for cooperation or respect.

You add speed to the conscious creating process in two ways. First, when you give a want more attention, you speed up its arrival. The more you think the thought, see it happening in your mind, and expect it, the sooner it appears.

The second way you add speed to the conscious creation process is to wrap your desire in emotions. Positive emotion quickens the appearance of positive wants. Likewise, negative emotion quickens the appearance of negative wants.

If you want a home or classroom that has a relaxed atmosphere, it is necessary to think thoughts of what you want. When you think those thoughts, add emotionality by feeling what it be like to have that desire manifest. Imagine how peaceful it would feel to have a relaxed atmosphere. Feel good about your ability to create it. Enjoy those positive feelings.

Also give attention to the times when you did notice a relaxed calmness in operation in your home or classroom. Revisit the emotion of those moments and enjoy them. Let all the positive emotion in and feel it from the top of your head to the tip of your toes. Savor it.

If you notice negative emotion arising as you anticipate making a transition from one activity to another, stop. Use that emotion as feedback and gently switch your thoughts to something you do want or to a time when your desire for a smooth transition was present.

Use negative emotion as a signal that it is time to change. It is time to change your thoughts, time to shift your attention, and time to refocus your energy.

Contrast

Many of us, parents and teachers included, are good at figuring out what we don't want.

"I don't want sloppy papers."

"I don't want students talking when I'm lecturing."
"I don't want my children taking my tools and
  leaving them all over the yard."
"I don't want my kids to gossip."
"I don't want to hear put-downs."
"I don't want to listen to that whining."

What you don't want is easily identified because when you see or hear the behaviors you don't like, you don't feel good and your mood is not positive. All of that negativity is easily recognizable.

The phenomenon of noticing what you don't want is called "contrast." The feeling, the sound, or the sight of what you don't want is in direct contrast to what you do want.

If you complain or even talk about what you don't want, you attract more of it into your life. In many schools the teachers' room is a prime center of conscious creation. When teachers convene in that location and complain about the administration, a parent, or a student, they are attracting more of the same. Likewise, if they use the teachers' room to celebrate successes, appreciate small gains, or affirm what has been accomplished, they attract more of that.

What do you tell your child's grandmother on the telephone? Does your conversation criticize Roberto's ineffective math teacher? Or do you inform her of his steady growth in hitting and catching a baseball? Whether you are talking about positive or negative situations, you are creating and attracting.

Even the act of simply noticing contrast sends out a negative vibration. So pay attention to what you are paying attention to in your classroom or home. That attention is vibrating.

Using Contrast

There is one way in which contrast is helpful. It can be useful in pointing to what you do want.

If you become aware that you don't want students turning in sloppy papers, immediately ask yourself, "If that's what I don't want, what is the opposite? What is it that I do want?"

- If you don't want sloppy papers, then you may want students turning in neat papers that are legible and spaced appropriately.

- If you don't want students talking when you are lecturing, then you probably want them listening and taking notes during those times.

- If you don't want your children taking your tools without putting them back when they are done, then you want your children to return your tools to their proper place immediately after they use them.

- If you don't want your kids to gossip, then perhaps you want them to speak about other people only in their presence.

- If you don't want to hear put-downs, then you want to hear children speaking respectfully.

- If don't want whining, then you want children asking for what they want in a clear, normal voice and tone.

So contrast can be useful in determining what you do want. It is important, however, to quickly note the contrast and get off the negative vibration of what you don't want as quickly as possible. Every moment you dwell on contrast you are placing your energy and attention on the negative.

Revisiting Wants

So what do you want in your teaching or parenting life? It is helpful to invest some time bringing clarity to your answer to this question.

Marty, a thirty-two-year-old mother of two, constructed this list of wants at one of our parent trainings.

1. I want a close relationship with my children.
2. I want to feel good about the way I parent.
3. I want to be in harmony with my spouse and create a great team.
4. I want to raise responsible, happy, confident children.
5. I want to model the message I am teaching my children.
6. I want to be solution oriented and invest my time in solving the problems that occur.
7. I want to create a culture of accountability in my family in a loving way with an open heart.
8. I want to help my children develop their inner authority.

9. I want to help my children learn the Attraction Principle.
10. I want to make myself dispensable so my children can take increasing amounts of control over their own lives.

Tevi, a fifteen-year teaching veteran, created the following want list.

1. I want students to learn the major concepts I am teaching.
2. I want to be energetic, enthusiastic, and in love with social studies.
3. I want to connect to all my students and feel a warm bond with them.
4. I want students to show enthusiasm and interest in social studies.
5. I want to teach to all the different learning styles.
6. I want to touch the spirit of my students and empower them to be all they can be.
7. I want to help my students see themselves as able, capable, and responsible.
8. I want self-responsible, self-motivated learners.
9. I want to help my students develop an appreciation for diversity.
10. I want to inspire and uplift my students to achieve more than they ever thought possible.

You may write, "I want self-responsible, self-motivated learners," and then immediately think, "I'll never be able to do that with this rowdy group." You may record on paper, "I want to be in harmony with my spouse and create a great team," and instantly remember that your spouse is a screamer and you aren't. You may even recall the argument you had about that recently.

When that happens, doubt has entered the scene. The presence of doubt delays or inhibits the arrival of your desire. Doubt is the signal that communicates you are not in the state of allowing.

Allowing

Allowing occurs only in the absence of doubt. When you experience doubt, you are not allowing your desire to reach you.

Allowing is in place when you hear yourself say:

"I think I can have this."
"This really is possible."
"It's already happening."
"It's on its way."

Limiting beliefs are the main source of doubt and resistance. You may believe:

- My child will never go to college.
- This is the worst class in the school.
- I'm a lousy parent.
- It's not possible to connect with every student.
- My children can't function without me.
- These students don't care about anything but TV, video games, and socializing.

You can tell if limiting beliefs are preventing your desire from appearing when you write or state the desire. When you write, "I want to be solution oriented and invest my time in solving the problems that occur," listen to the self-talk that is generated immediately following that desire. If you hear yourself say, "But I can't because . . .," you have made an important discovery. What follows the "I can't because . . ." is your limiting belief.

"I want self-responsible, self-motivated learners, <u>but it won't happen because the parents don't reinforce that at home</u>" points to your limiting belief.

"I want to help my children learn the Attraction Principle, <u>but I don't have the necessary skills</u>" reveals the belief that is holding you back from reaching your desire. You don't think you have the necessary skills.

When you identify a limiting belief, you are on your way to allowing your desire to come to you. Recognizing the limiting belief is the first step. Next, it is time to design allowing statements.

Allowing Statements

Deactivating your limiting belief requires the construction of "allowing statements." An allowing statement allows you to successfully alter the limiting belief by challenging its validity. This procedure involves two steps.

1. Think about all the people in the entire world. Ask yourself if what you want has ever been accomplished by any one of them. Is it possible that anyone accomplished it this week or this year? In all of time?

2. When you discover the answer to the questions

above is "yes," construct allowing statements that state those conditions. Make sure your allowing statements describe the accomplishments of other people.

If your limiting belief is, "I don't have the necessary skills to teach the Attraction Principle to my children," challenge that belief with allowing statements.

- Many people all over the world are teaching the Attraction Principle to their children.
- Some people are teaching the Attraction Principle to their children today.
- Many of those people did not know how to do it when they began.
- Many people are currently discovering how to teach the Attraction Principle to their children.
- Other parents have found resources to help them teach the Attraction Principle to their children.
- Some parents are reading one of those resources at this precise moment.

Because your allowing statements are all true, creating and then reading them will enable you to lessen or remove the doubt that surrounds your important teaching or parenting desire. Allowing statements spawn hope and the belief that your desire is indeed possible.

To further reduce doubt and activate the allowing process to work on manifesting your desire, you can choose from several strategies. These include visualization, writing affirmations, pretending, and anticipating.

Positive Picturing

Positive picturing, or "mental rehearsal" as it is sometimes called, can help you eliminate doubt and attract your parenting or teaching desire. This technique asks you to use your imagination to picture the positive process and outcome of a desire. It is a mental run-through of what you want to do or create.

If you don't believe in the power of images, interview an advertising executive who pays millions of dollars for a thirty-second commercial during the televising of the Super Bowl. Ask her if images can influence behavior.

The universe doesn't care if the thought you think is really happening or if you are creating it in your imagination. The Attraction Principle works either way. Creating a mental picture in your head of what you want helps you to focus on the end result rather than on *what is.* Adding positive emotion to that image makes it even stronger.

Perhaps you and your spouse don't agree on parenting issues right now. You can imagine it, though. Begin your picturing session as if you can see it happening. In your mind, watch the two of you discussing an important issue. Notice how you listen to each other and clarify points of view before you move on. Notice how both of you react when you feel listened to and valued. See yourselves getting closer to consensus and to each other. If you picture a negative result, simply put your imagination on rewind. Back up a few spaces and rerun the picture. In your mind, create the outcome exactly as you would like it to be.

Feel strong, positive emotions as you do this mental rehearsal. Be happy with yourself. Feel confident and successful. Notice the positive feelings reflected on your spouse's face as well.

When you have finished, go on about your day knowing that you are one step closer to materializing your desire.

A vision board or vision journal is another way to plant positive pictures in your mind. Cut pictures from magazines or use real photographs of your children or students to show images of what you want to create.

Display that photo that shows the time your son and daughter cooperated to wash both of their bicycles. Put up the photo that shows the family walking together holding hands. Post the A spelling paper your child brought home from school. Put up the award your daughter got at camp. Display items that show your children as confident, able, and responsible.

Educators, create a scrapbook/journal that shows samples and incidents of your desires being met. Add pictures of you being enthusiastic and energetic as you share your love of your subject matter. Include pictures, drawings, or photographs that show teachers bonding with their students. Show students being engaged and interested. Record examples of activities you have designed that touch different learning styles. Add the note that the substitute teacher left saying how much fun it was for her to teach your class for a day. If you don't have one, make one up.

Begin each day reviewing your journal. Feel the positive feelings that come with knowing what you desire is on its way to your classroom.

Affirmations

An affirmation is a positive thought you intentionally choose to place in your mind to produce a desired result. Some examples follow.

- I have a close relationship with my children.
- I am in harmony with my spouse and we are a great parenting team.
- I raise responsible, happy, confident children.
- I help my children develop their inner authority.
- My students learn the major concepts I am teaching.
- I teach to all the different learning styles.
- I touch the spirit of my students and empower them to be all they can be.
- I help my students see themselves as able, capable, and responsible.
- I inspire and uplift my students to achieve more than they ever thought possible.

The use of affirmations is a way to reprogram your mind through repetitious thought. Thoughts have energy. The vibrational energy from an affirmation goes out into the world, has an impact on people and objects, and attracts situations and circumstances that have similar vibrational energy patterns.

The key to an effective use of affirmations is to remember that the Attraction Principle is not responding to your words. It is responding to your emotion, the vibrational energy behind those words.

Many affirmations do not work. Perhaps you have found yourself repeating, "I have a close relationship with all my students," only to discover that two of your students remain distant and appear unapproachable. What is going on there?

The Attraction Principle is not responding to your words because they are not true for you. When you write or say them, you know they are not true. Knowing that, your affirmations are wrapped in negative emotionality and sent out into the world with negative vibrations.

For affirmations to work, they have to be accurate. They must be true for you in this moment. "I have a close relationship with all my students" is not true. Part of you knows this and says back to yourself, "No you don't! Who are you trying to fool?"

To create an affirmation that generates positive emotion you have to design one that is true. We suggest you consider some of the following sentence starters when constructing your affirmations.

- I am creating . . .
- I am in the process of . . .
- _____ is appearing in my life more and more.
- I am currently attracting . . .

Maybe you do not have a close relationship with all your students. Regardless, you are creating it at this very moment. Perhaps it's not true that you are in harmony with your spouse and that you are currently a great parenting team. It is true that you are in the process of creating harmony with your spouse and are becoming a great parenting team.

When you construct an affirmation that is true for you, you will feel positive emotion. You can then be certain that your affirmation is sending out the vibration that is attracting your desire.

Act As If

Perhaps you do not believe that you currently inspire and uplift your students to achieve more than they ever thought possible. Then act as if you do! Pretend you are inspiring your students. Be the lead actor in a movie starring yourself and your students. Play out that leading role as if you are the star of the production.

Act as if everything you say is being taken in by your students and added to their long-term memory banks. Pretend that your students can't wait to get to your class. Act as if they appreciate every effort you make to teach to all their unique learning styles.

Find a colleague or another parent to participate in a weekly conversation where you agree to *talk as if* your desire has already manifested. This can be done in person or on the phone.

A typical *talk as if* conversation might sound like this.

➢ You: "Hello, Reuben."

➢ Friend: "Oh, hi, Gabriella. How's it going?"

➢ You: "I have some good news. My youngest son, Paco, made the honor roll this marking period."

➢ Friend: "That is good news."

➢ You: "Yeah, this is his first time, and he seems to be as excited as I am. I'm so proud for him. He has worked his tail off to make it happen."

➢ Friend: "How did he do it?"

➢ You: "Persistence, mainly. He did some extra credit in two classes and had a tutor for math. He basically did it himself with effort and determination."

➢ Friend: "Remember how you used to worry about him?"

➢ You: "I sure do. I feel kind of silly now thinking about it. I'm glad I learned that worry sends out negative vibrations and attracts what I don't want. I'm sure happy I read *Teaching The ATTRACTION PRINCIPLE™ to Children* a couple of years ago. It was the catalyst that began this incredible change in all of our lives."

➢ Friend: "Yes, and I appreciate your buying me a copy, too. My classroom has become much more peaceful in the last year. My students are more interested. They pay attention in class better. And we're all having more fun."

➤ You: "That's great, Gabriella."

➤ Friend: "Reuben, it feels so good to know that I'm touching the spirit of so many students. Many of them come to me needing to be uplifted, affirmed, and appreciated. I am able to do that for them and I can see the positive effects it has on them. It's thrilling to watch them bloom and grow."

➤ You: "That's exactly how I feel about Paco. What an honor it is to be able to watch him grow into the fine young man he is becoming. He is maturing and becoming self-responsible right before my eyes."

➤ Friend: "Hey, I have to go now. My first-hour class is starting soon and many of my students get there early so they can do some extra work on their projects. Talk to you soon."

➤ You: "Okay, will do. Bye."

Act as if, talk as if, dress as if, think as if, and carry yourself as if. Be who you intend to be. And do it now, even if it's an act.

Purposeful Anticipation

Purposefully anticipating positive outcomes with your thoughts and emotions launches your desire into the universe. As you continue to move through your parenting or teaching life, expect that your desire will materialize.

Purposeful anticipation activates your desire and sends it on its way to you. Thinking, visualizing, acting as if, and purposefully expecting your desire is a powerful combination. Follow that path and the actions you take will lead you to your destination.

We were recently challenged by a parent who told us, "I'll believe it when I see it," referring to his son's degree of responsibility. We challenged him to turn the statement around so that it became, "I'll see it when I believe it." You can choose to play the parenting or teaching game with either statement. Which statement do you believe? Which one do you think will get you to where you want to be?

Use Surprise

John Clayton received a call from his son's principal the fourth week of his fifth-grade year. "Sammy is in my office," said the administrator. "He used the F-word in class and I've suspended him for two days. Please come and get him as soon as possible."

John had a thirty-minute drive from work to the elementary school where the incident occurred. Although he thought about it the entire time, he had reached no decision about what to do or say to his son by the time he pulled into the parking lot.

Not having any clear directions about what to say or do, John remained silent when his son got in the car. After several miles had passed, Sammy asked, "Did you hear what I said in class?" "Yep," replied the disappointed father. "What are you going to do about it?" queried Sammy. That's when this parent used "surprise talk" to clearly communicate how he viewed his son.

"I'm not sure what I'm going to do," John said. "Actually, I'm too stunned to react right now. The whole incident has taken me by surprise. It's not anything I ever expected so I need to think about it awhile. We can talk about it after dinner tonight when I've had time to process it a bit."

What this father did by using surprise talk was let his son know he did not see him as someone who would use inappropriate language in school. In fact, the behavior was so unexpected that he didn't have a plan in place for how to deal with it. The real message he sent his son was, "I don't expect that type of behavior from you."

Some parents and teachers use surprise talk to communicate negative expectations.

"Got in trouble again, eh? I'm not surprised."
"Didn't do your chores? I might have expected that from you."
"I could have predicted you were the one that started the argument."

When you use surprise talk, you are communicating expectations. One of the best things you can do for your child or student is to expect their success and communicate that to them.

Giving

One frequent criticism we hear of the Attraction Principle is that it's all about getting. People use it to get wealthy, healthy, a new job, a soul mate, a new house, furniture, a boat, and so on. Indeed, the Attraction Principle works well for manifesting the material things in your life.

The Attraction Principle also works for giving. You can use it to give love, attention, time, and energy. An educator attending one of our seminars built the following want list during one of our interactive activities.

- I want to give my students confidence.
- I want to give my students an appreciation of great literature.
- I want to give my students critical thinking skills.
- I want to give my students positive energy when I am with them.
- I want to give my students opportunities to challenge authority and state their own views respectfully.
- I want to give my students the ability to see situations from different perspectives.
- I want to give my students the real me because it is the best thing I have to offer them.

Action

When a student swears in your classroom, action is needed. If paint gets spilled, equipment is disrespected, or teasing takes place, action is called for. Action is also necessary to create a positive relationship or a caring atmosphere or to encourage positive attitudes in your children and students.

To ensure that the action you take produces positive vibrations and emotions, make sure you have laid the proper groundwork prior to taking action. By setting forth the thoughts, images, and emotions in advance, using the techniques described in this book, you create the foundation from which your actions will have maximum impact.

There is no amount of action you can take as a parent or as a teacher that can overcome a foundation of negative thought and emotion. All the action in the world will not get you where you want to go if you haven't taken the time to create the leverage that comes from wanting, expecting, and allowing.

To make sure your actions flow from positive thoughts and images, move UP before you move IN.

Move UP Before You Move IN

When your third-grader spills paint, when your eighth-grader uses inappropriate language, when your own child burps loudly at the dinner table - action is called for. To ensure that the action you take flows from love as well as from logic, pause. Take three deep breaths and actively change your frame of mind before you respond. Move UP in your consciousness before you move IN with action.

To help you move UP before you move IN, we recommend five strategies.

1. Make a BE choice before you make a DO choice.
2. Talk to yourself before you talk to the child.

3. See it all as perfect.
4. Accept that *what is* is.
5. Make no assumptions.

1. <u>Make a BE choice before you make a DO choice.</u>

As educators and parents, we make DO choices regularly. Activities we sometimes decide to do with our students or children include reading a story, giving assignments, reassigning seats, and distributing chores. We are all familiar with making a DO choice. Not as familiar to many adults is the concept of making a BE choice. A BE choice occurs when you purposefully choose how you are going to BE when you do whatever it is that you decide to do.

When reading a story, for instance, you could choose to BE silly, emphatic, serious, demonstrative, quick, humorous, childlike, or lively. How you choose to BE will dramatically alter the experience of the story. If you don't think so, be silly one time and serious the next. You will feel and see the difference and the impact each choice has on your students or children.

If the task is to discuss poor grades on a report card with your child, that's your DO choice. We suggest you decide how you want to BE before you activate your DO choice of engaging in the discussion. You might choose to be firm, confrontational, empathetic, sincere, friendly, loving, surprised, thorough, open-minded, or inquisitive. By making a BE choice, you shape your experience of discussing the report card. Your behavior will flow from your choice of how to BE and adjust to fit that form. In essence, you have managed your mind to create a desired result.

2. <u>Talk to yourself before you talk to the child.</u>

By paying attention to your thoughts and purposefully shaping the conversation you have with yourself, you take charge of your attitude, your energy, and your relationship to the teaching moment that is before you.

Using encouraging self-talk is one way to effectively take charge and manage your own mind. Encouraging self-talk helps you to create the frame of mind you desire rather than leave that important function to chance. For example, you might choose to tell yourself:

> "I don't have to take this personally. The student's choices do not mean that I'm a good teacher or a bad one. This isn't about me. It's about him and where he currently is on the learning curve."

> "This behavior is age appropriate. Ten-year-olds tease and taunt, and little kids wiggle. Teenagers activate power struggles. Even though I don't like this particular behavior, it's normal for the child's age."

> "Helpful lessons spring from uncomfortable situations. This situation has the potential to create learning and healing for me and for this youngster."

Refuse to let whatever thoughts initially spring into your mind control you when a potentially stressful parenting or teaching situation presents itself. Notice your thoughts and change them if you choose. You can rise above any situation and bring calm and peace to it by using helpful self-talk.

3. <u>See it all as perfect.</u>

Another mind management technique you can use to move UP in your consciousness is to choose to see your present circumstance as perfect.

If you have a family gathering and your daughter speaks respectfully to her grandfather, it's perfect. If you have a family gathering and your daughter speaks disrespectfully to her grandfather, that's perfect, too. Your daughter is providing you with the data you need to help you create the perfect learning experience or design the perfect debriefing questions to help her examine the issue of respect and her choices surrounding it.

If all your students pass the chapter test on Westward Expansion, that's perfect. If half your students bomb the test, that too is perfect. You now have the perfect information you need to design the perfect logical consequence resulting from their decision concerning the amount of time relegated to study.

Choose to view these parenting and teaching events as opportunities for you to practice moving UP before you move IN. They are the perfect situations you need to help you practice this skill. Welcome them and you will keep your vibrations positive.

4. <u>Accept that *what is* is.</u>

Another Move UP before you move IN technique is to accept that *what is* is. If you find yourself thinking that things should be other than they are - that your students should be different, that your children should know better, or that you should have done something differently - you are emotionally resisting and fighting *what is*.

The fact is that your kindergarten students did decorate the bathroom wall with permanent markers. That's *what is*. The wall is the wall and it is covered with permanent marker.

Yes, work to make changes on the physical level. Teach the necessary lessons to encourage that different markers be used on a different surface next time. Involve your students in cleanup. Implement appropriate consequences if necessary. Dealing with the situation on the physical level is important and necessary - and that part of teaching can be handled more effectively when you emotionally accept your present-moment circumstances.

5. <u>Make no assumptions.</u>

Beware of the assumption trap. As adults, we think we know. We think we know why the student lied to us. We think we know what our teen is thinking. We think we know what our preschooler is about to do next. We think we know who began the argument in the cooperative group. To move UP before you move IN, free your mind of assumptions.

Allowing assumptions to control your mind leads to conflict and misunderstanding. To manage your mind effectively in important parenting or teaching situations it's necessary to refrain from making assumptions. Tell yourself: "I may not know for sure what is going on here. I will keep an open mind. Understanding is my top priority." Keep your commitment to manage your mind first by entering crucial parenting moments free of assumptions.

When you use the Move UP before you move IN strategies, you keep your thoughts positive. You manage your mind so that you manage your emotions. When you take action from a positive frame of mind, feeling positive emotions, you ensure that the action you take flows from your picture and desire of who you want to be as a parent or teacher.

Gratitude

Another way to send out strong positive vibrations is through appreciation. Be grateful for small signs that your desire is coming. If your child completes his math assignment, be grateful. If your daughter tells your grandfather what she learned and what she intends to do differently next time, be grateful.

If your teen calls to tell you he will be home late, be grateful. You can concentrate on the fact that he didn't get home on time or you can appreciate that he called you. The choice is yours. The choice you make will determine the vibrations you send into the universe.

What are you thankful for as an educator or parent? Keep an appreciation journal. Feel good as you watch it grow over time. Enjoy the positive emotions that flow from each reading of your collection of appreciations.

It is helpful to appreciate situations that don't appear at first glance to be useful or valuable. For instance, why not be thankful that your child is two years behind grade level in his reading ability? This struggling reader is giving you the opportunity to read to him regularly at night. This evening ritual will help build connectedness between you and your child while at the same time modeling your love for the printed word. Great literature can be shared as you simultaneously bond with your child. This opportunity is an incredible blessing. Appreciate it.

Why not be thankful that your daughter's soccer team lost their last game? It is important that your children have experiences of both winning and losing. By losing, children have the opportunity to learn to handle defeat and bounce back next time. With your help, they can learn that winning or losing is not the measure of who and what they are as human beings. They can learn they are more than the score. They can learn that it's effort, energy, and playing up to potential with good sportsmanship that defines a winner, not the scoreboard. Appreciate the opportunity the loss brings and be grateful for it.

Why not be thankful that your teenager received a speeding ticket for going forty-five miles per hour in a twenty-five mile per hour speed zone? Getting a ticket is not a bad thing. Not if your teen learns from it and slows her driving for the next year. If she takes personal responsibility, pays the ticket, and is more cautious about her driving, the ticket may well save her life or the life of someone else in the future. Bless the ticket and give thanks for its blessings.

Why not be thankful for sibling rivalry? "He got more

than I did" and "It isn't fair" are common childhood refrains. Hitting, poking, and teasing a sister are typical childhood behaviors. Bless these opportunities to help your children learn how to get along with each other. Use them as times to teach interpersonal skills and the importance of touching each other gently. Sibling rivalry is a call for help, a signal that your children need lessons in how to interact positively with each other. Bless their unskillful way of asking for help. Be grateful that you recognize it and help them grow in working and playing cooperatively.

Why not be thankful that your adolescent asked you about oral sex? This is a great sign. It means your child trusts you enough to talk to you about sex. It means she is not getting all her sex knowledge from the street. It means you have been taking your role as sex educator in your family seriously and that you have moved beyond "the Talk" to having an ongoing, honest conversation about the important subject of sex. Congratulate yourself. It is a blessing that you are willing to fulfill that role for your child and that she is responding to it positively. Give thanks.

Why not be thankful for your special-needs student? Do you have a student with ADHD, one who is autistic or dyslexic? Does your student have Down syndrome? Your students are in your life for a reason. Perhaps they have come to help you learn patience, understanding, or commitment. Perhaps they are here to teach you and the other students in your classroom about tolerance, acceptance of differences, or unconditional love. Their presence is a blessing. Be thankful for the contribution they are making to the planet and to your classroom.

Keep It a Secret

Not all people will be supportive of your desire to become the parent or teacher you always wanted to be. There are some who will not be supportive and who will spill negative energy onto your dreams.

Never share your plans with people unless you are absolutely sure they will be supportive. Negative people will tell you to "get real!" They will laugh at you for thinking you can inspire students to love geometry or world history. Some will mock you for thinking your teen will tell you the truth. Their words can plant doubt in your mind. With these people it is best to keep your desires a secret.

More than one professional educator has told us they have made a decision to stay out of the teachers' lounge permanently. Some even choose to eat lunch with the kids rather than listen to the negative verbiage spewed out where the teachers gather to eat.

Gather like-minded teachers in your room to share lunch and positive expectations. Create a mastermind group. Locate the people who think like you do. Create a Thursday morning coffee club date with them. Listen to and support each other's dreams. Seek solutions, celebrate successes, realize your dreams together.

Allowing Revisited

It is easier to change your own behavior than that of your children or students. You cannot create their experience for them because you cannot think their thoughts. You cannot inject them with an emotion. Children make their own interpretations of the events of their lives. They do this in the privacy of their own minds, in thinking their own thoughts, and in feeling their own feelings.

That being the case, it is important that you assume the stance that you are in charge of you and they are in charge of them. We are talking about allowing your children to be that which they want to be, allowing them to grow into that which they will become, allowing them to learn their lessons rather than yours.

- Can you respect your children's right to choose and not judge them even as you hold them accountable for their actions?

- Can you feel positive emotion from knowing your students are learning about cause and effect?

- Can you suspend judgment until you see how the lesson is used?

- Can you refrain from making your children or students wrong even as you hold them accountable?

- Can you allow them to use their own solution instead of yours?

True allowing is concentrating on yourself, maintaining your own center, your own happiness, no matter what your children or students are doing. Can you find peace when they are creating chaos? Can you be the center that holds when change and confusion swirls around you?

You will know that allowing is in place in your parenting or teaching life when you can allow your children to create whatever they want or don't want without feeling negative emotion about it. It is from this space that you can best begin to offer lessons that help the important children in your life learn the Attraction Principle.

SECTION TWO

There is no big secret to teaching the Attraction Principle to children. You teach it the same way you would teach anything else you want your child or student to learn. Consider the father who wants to teach his daughter to hit a softball. At the very least, he must:

- Make a decision and a commitment to teach her.
- Invest regular time and energy in the project.
- Talk about and demonstrate hitting.
- Pitch the ball so his daughter can practice hitting.
- Give positive and corrective feedback as needed.
- Practice again and again on a regular basis.

Your children will not learn the Attraction Principle unless you make a purposeful decision and commitment to teach them. This will require that you regularly invest time and energy in the project. You will need to talk about and demonstrate how you use the Attraction Principle in your own life. You will have to stay alert for opportunities (teachable moments) to draw attention to situations that illustrate the

Attraction Principle and people creating their own reality in action.

Teaching the Attraction Principle will require you to return to the concept again and again as your children move through the ages and stages of normal childhood development. Positive and corrective feedback will be needed regularly. Likewise, debriefing, the processing of life's unfolding situations, will often be necessary.

In short, to learn the Attraction Principle your children or students need an adult who values the content, uses it in his or her own life, and makes a commitment to teach it to others.

Your Role

Are you a parent? If so, one of your main jobs is to teach values and life skills to your children. You are their first and most important teacher. You, more than any other adult, determine what is important for them to learn.

Are you a teacher? If so, someone else has likely decided what is important for your students to learn. The Attraction Principle is probably not in your third-grade curriculum guide. Nor is the probability high that it will be found on the list of exit outcomes necessary to pass a class in your high school. Regardless, you are a professional educator, uniquely qualified to make moment-to-moment decisions about what to add and what to leave out of the curriculum.

Our position is this: Whether you are a parent or an educator, see the Attraction Principle as part of your curriculum. Realize it is an integral part of the values and life skills that every child needs to know in order to grow and evolve into what and who they want to be.

Think of it this way: The Attraction Principle is a bonus. Other parents are teaching values. So their children learn values. You are teaching values plus the Attraction Principle.

Your children get an added value, one they can use their entire lives to intentionally create their own life experiences.

Other teachers are teaching math, science, or language arts. Therefore, their students are receiving math, science, and language arts. Your students, on the other hand, are receiving a bonus. They get math, science, or language arts plus the Attraction Principle.

Because you are their teacher, they receive a way of looking at and experiencing life that leaves them empowered and in control of the reality they are creating for themselves.

Whether you are a teacher or a parent, there are two ways to teach the Attraction Principle.

One is to purposefully design lessons around the concepts. You intentionally design a specific lesson to help children learn a concept, technique, or strategy related to the Attraction Principle.

That's what Randy Wilson did recently.

Randy, Martha, and their three children - Emily, age eight; Eric, age eleven; and Erin, age fourteen - gathered in the living room for family video night. Once a month the entire family watches a DVD together. This is an expected and anticipated family ritual that has been in place for the past six years.

The video selection, usually from the Spiritual Cinema Circle, is viewed by the entire family. The routine includes making and consuming popcorn and special orange juice smoothies during the viewing. On this night the selection was **The Secret**, *the ninety-minute DVD that popularized the Law of Attraction.*

Not much was said during the showing of the video as family members munched on popcorn and listened and watched intently. When the movie was over, the family gathered at the kitchen table to offer opinions, feelings, and thoughts. Each person was given the opportunity to comment on **The Secret**. *All of them took the opportunity.*

Mr. Wilson structured the discussion period with a few questions to stimulate thinking and conversation.

"What interested you the most about **The Secret**?*"*

"How do you see yourself using **The Secret** *in your life?"*

"In what ways, if any, are you skeptical about **The Secret**?*"*

"If you could use the Law of Attraction in your life right now, what would you want to create?"

"Can you recall incidents where you already used the Law of Attraction in your life and you didn't realize it until now? Tell us about them."

"What is one way you plan to use the Law of Attraction this week?"

The Wilson family spent an additional hour processing what each person had learned and how they planned to use it. They concluded the session by agreeing to come back the following Sunday night to share their individual experiences of using what they had learned.

Randy Wilson took the lead in his family and purposefully created this lesson to introduce his children to the concepts inherent in *The Secret.* He recognizes that this was only the first lesson and that many more will be necessary before his children fully implement these important concepts. But, thanks to his effort, the Secret is no longer a secret to his children.

The second way to teach the Attraction Principle involves no planning. It requires no designed lessons. It asks for no preparation or purchase of special materials. It simply asks you to stay conscious about teaching this concept to children. Always be looking for a teachable moment. Use what the universe brings you to teach important lessons.

The teaching of the Attraction Principle comes in many little pieces that are not always sequential. Be alert for those opportunities. That's what Stella Valdez did with a fourth-grade student.

"I don't want to go out for recess," complained one of

Stella's students recently as the other kids rapidly made their exit to the playground.

"How come?" Stella asked, not yet recognizing this as an opportunity to teach what she liked to call "the silent curriculum." She named it the silent curriculum because she doesn't talk much about it to others. It isn't written down like the traditional fourth-grade curriculum. This curriculum is her private secret.

"'Cause I don't want to," the boy responded.

The student's second uttering of "I don't" was the trigger that alerted Stella to the opportunity to teach the silent curriculum.

"If you don't want to go out, what do you want to do?" she queried.

"I want to stay in and finish my report on bugs. I'm almost done and I want to add the cover."

"I understand now," Stella remarked. "Telling me what you want rather than what you don't want helps me see your desire more clearly. You have a much better chance of getting it that way. Yes, you can stay in today."

Stella Valdez began this particular morning with no specific intention to teach to her silent curriculum. Yet, when the opportunity presented itself, she jumped on it. "Telling me what you want rather than what you don't want helps me see your desire more clearly. You have a much better chance of getting it that way" planted a seed. In time, this student will come to understand that when he is clear about what he wants, he too will see it more clearly and have a much better chance of attracting it into his life.

Like showing a DVD or talking about wants, the activities and ideas on the following pages are not difficult. Most of them simply require staying conscious, making teaching the Attraction Principle a priority, and investing the time necessary to do it. That's what you do when you are teaching your students to read or helping your child learn to ride a bike. Why not do it with how to create the world they desire?

The Attraction Principle

The Attraction Principle is not unlike the principles governing gravity, magnetism, and electricity. All are unseen as they are happening. What is visible are the results of gravity, magnetism, and electricity. The same holds true for the Attraction Principle.

We teach children to keep their fingers out of light sockets because of the effects of electricity. We teach them to step carefully as they climb trees because of the Gravity Principle. We teach them how to roam a sandy beach with a metal detector discovering treasures that are invisible to the eye using the Magnetism Principle.

Explaining gravity, magnetism, and electricity to children is something many adults do. If children are too young to conceptualize the processes, they catch on to the effects soon enough.

You can explain the Attraction Principle to children

the same way you explain gravity, magnetism, or electricity. Some children will be skeptical. Some will think you went insane. Others will be open to the possibility. Some will realize with an inner knowing that you speak the truth.

Don't overreact if children don't immediately embrace your teachings. You have all year to demonstrate and reveal these concepts if you are a teacher and many years if you are a parent.

Put posters and sayings around your classroom or house to promote curiosity.

- Dream big.
- If you think you can, you can.
- Thoughts are things.
- We create our own reality.
- I am a mental magnet.
- I am an attraction machine.
- You can make your crystal ball say whatever you want it to.

If children ask about the sayings, explain what they mean and your reason for posting them on the walls.

Show your children or students an example of an airplane and then trace it back to the plans the Wright Brothers had. Show them how an airplane first began as a thought, then became a plan, then bloomed into reality. Do the same with a guitar, a chair, an elevator, or an ink pen.

Be alert for opportunities to teach the Attraction Principle that seemingly fall into your lap or "show up out of the blue."

Jason McWalters won the conference wrestling championship as a junior in high school. When asked how he did it, he replied, "I've been thinking about doing it for five years."

Mrs. Barker brought a banker to school to talk to her sixth-grade class about saving and credit. When asked where money comes from, the speaker gave an unexpected answer. "It shows up in your life when you think about it a lot and then take action."

"How did we end up with a nice house like this?" Billy Canada asked his father.

Billy's father, Mrs. Barker, and Jason's wrestling coach were each presented with an opportunity to teach a piece of the Attraction Principle. Whether or not they use the opportunity depends on if they recognize it, are willing to invest the time, and are committed to the process. If they are alert and willing, they can each use this teachable moment to point out to other youngsters how thoughts do indeed turn into reality.

Vibrations

Scientists tell us that everything is vibrating. The tiniest of atoms is vibrating. Even a desk, which appears solid, is made up of atoms that are moving.

Song and music are based on vibration. The vocal chords vibrate. So do the strings on a guitar. A father at one of our recent workshops told the following tale.

"I recently took my children to a symphony celebration for children," he told us. "It was an incredible experience. Both my children, ages three and six, were enthralled by this group of musicians."

The musicians let the children touch, play, and then feel the vibrations of each instrument in the orchestra. What made the experience even more powerful was that they talked to the children about the vibrations of all things, not just musical instruments. They explained how everything living and not living, including thoughts and feelings, creates a vibration in the world. Some of these vibrations we can feel easily, like the base drum; some are less noticeable, like a tiny chime.

They had the children go inside themselves and become aware of the different vibrations they feel when an instrument is played and then when a word is said. The musicians would play a harsh-sounding note, let the children feel it, and then correlate the note with harsh-sounding words and let the children feel that, too. A soft note was compared to soft words.

That trip to the symphony occurred five years ago. To this day, this father still uses those musical examples when talking to his children about the importance of vibrations. "They still remember the feelings those sounds generated," he told us. "Because of that experience I am able to talk to my children more easily about some of the concepts you presented in your workshop here today, especially the part about vibrating with the universe."

So maybe you don't have an enlightened symphony orchestra in your community to share with your students or family. Then bring a tuning fork into your classroom or home. Demonstrate the vibration. Have your children take turns vibrating the fork. Inform them that this same concept applies to thoughts and sends those thoughts out into the universe. Do the same with a guitar, base fiddle, or violin.

Have children experience the concept of vibrations by putting a rubber band between their thumb and forefinger. Have them snap the rubber band to produce the vibration.

Get a glass (not plastic) and wet your finger. Circle the top of the glass over and over with your finger until you make it ring. Have your children or students take a turn making it vibrate.

The point here is that everything in the universe has a vibration. When you see a road sign vibrating in a high wind, point it out. Do the same with a fan, waves on the ocean, or a drum.

When you do this, you are teaching children a crucial piece in understanding the Attraction Principle. Experiencing vibrations and being able to identify how they feel will later help children align with the vibrational essence of what the universe is singing.

Thoughts

It is through our thoughts that we make our world. Someone thought of a light bulb before it was made manifest. Someone else thought of crossing the Rocky Mountains in covered wagons. Someone thought slavery was a good idea. Someone thought going to the moon was possible. All have come to pass.

A seventeen-year teaching veteran, Connie Frederick, recently read The Little Engine That Could *to her class. She read every page with great enthusiasm, adding increased emphasis on the little engine's primary thought, "I think I can. I think I can. I think I can."*

Connie's students sat there mesmerized, hanging on every word, listening to the little engine's struggle. They followed along closely as their teacher showed them each page before she turned it and read on. Connie's primary goal was to help her students understand the importance of thoughts.

Adapted from *Spirit Whisperers: Teachers Who Nourish a Child's Spirit*, by Chick Moorman, Personal Power Press, www.personalpower-press.com.

As you read the preceding paragraph, did you picture an early-childhood classroom? If you did, you were holding an inaccurate picture. Connie Frederick is a high school English teacher who happens to believe that great literature comes in all kinds of shapes and packages.

The Little Engine That Could is not listed as an approved book in the curriculum guide for Connie's subject matter. When asked why she read that story, she said simply, "I want my students to learn that the greatest transportation system in the world is your train of thought."

Following the reading of *The Little Engine That Could,* Connie led a class discussion, invited journal writing, and assigned a personal response paper to be completed and turned in later in the week.

Teachers like Connie and parents with similar views know that teaching children the cause and effect relationship between thoughts and outcomes is more important than the date of the Boston Tea Party, which mammals lay eggs, or the definition of a circle. They realize that once a child grasps the throttle of her train of thought and actively experiences the power that comes from providing direction to her own life, there is no destination that is unavailable to that child.

Even small children can understand the connection between thought and outcomes if their caregivers help them appreciate it. Begin with these kinds of activities.

- Have your daughter think about the picture she wants to draw and then draw it.
- Have her think about what she wants for her birthday and write that in her journal.
- Have your son decide what he wants to have for supper and then help you make it.
- Have him think about the animal he would like to make out of clay and then create it.

Doing these kinds of activities is important. Processing them is even more important. After the child thinks of a picture and then draws it, it is valuable to help him connect the dots from thought (cause) to picture (effect). Your job is to help him become aware that he had to think it before it happened.

Older children can be challenged to uncover the thoughts that led to World War II, freeing the slaves, or building the Great Pyramid. These types of assignments make exciting social studies or language arts activities. They are also useful for discussion starters at the family dinner table.

Assign your students to consider what happens when they think that an assignment is going to be difficult. When you think this way, what usually happens? What if you think it is going to be easy? Debrief their reactions in an open discussion.

Parents can have these same kinds of discussions with their children. When you think you can't find the toy you are looking for, what usually happens? What if you thought you could do that math problem and took the next step? What do you think would happen after that? As parents it is important that we take the time to debrief our children's reactions and create an open discussion about the cause and effect nature of the world around them.

The Self-Fulfilling Prophecy

The self-fulfilling prophecy operates the same whether your child thinks that second grade will be easy or hard. If he thinks it will be hard, he will more likely notice the parts that are hard or interpret challenging aspects as difficult. Because he notices the hard parts, he stacks up supportive evidence in his consciousness and eventually proves his belief to himself. Sure enough, second grade does indeed become hard in his mind and in his world.

"So I should convince him that second grade is easy?" a mother questioned. "No," we told her, "because if you said that and he found it easy, he would think what he accomplished was only because it was easy." Instead, remind him about his strengths. Mention his persistence, degree of effort, and determination. Let him know that even though he thinks it is hard, he has attributes that will allow him to handle it successfully.

Once a week Gramma Stockwell spends the evening playing card games with her two grandsons, Mark and Hunter. One evening she stopped the game to remind Hunter of a very important concept.

"Hunter, when you keep saying, 'I never get the cards I need' you are telling the universe to never give you the cards you need."

"But Gramma, I keep getting terrible cards. I'm not going to win a single game tonight."

"You're correct. When you keep talking like that, bad cards are exactly what you will get."

"Gramma, it's not like I can control the cards that are being dealt."

"Not directly, but you can indirectly. It's called a self-fulfilling prophecy. When you believe something long enough, it just starts happening that way."

"So what can I do about it now? The cards I get are the cards I get. I can't change them."

"You can't change this hand, but when you change your thoughts about your future hands, you might be

surprised at what you get. Start by changing what you think and say about this hand. Say things like, 'This might not be the best hand, and I can be creative in how I play it.'"

Hunter's older brother piped in, "Have you ever heard of bluffing? That's just a creative way to play a poor hand."

Gramma continued, "Then, as the next hand is being dealt, say to yourself, 'No matter what hand I get, I know how to play it' or 'I can't wait for the next set of cards. They're just what I need to win this game.' Watch what happens. You just might be surprised."

Hunter nodded in partial agreement as Mark scooped up the cards and began shuffling.

It is not important that Hunter's cards immediately begin to change and that he wages a fierce comeback and wins the game. Much more important is that his grandmother gave him a valuable life lesson on how to think positively about the cards he had been dealt, or about himself and his ability to handle playing the game with those cards. He had just been given a valuable gift, a lesson about the way the self-fulfilling prophecy works.

"I'm not looking forward to today's soccer game," moaned Alberto. "This team is our worst enemy and the toughest team in the league."

"Hold on, Alberto," his father piped in as he drove down the road. "If you keep talking like that, you're

bound to have a tough game."

"Well, it's true."

"It might be true that the team you play today has a better record than your team. It is also true that the more you continue to say that they're your worst enemy and the toughest team, the more power you give them to stay that way. When you think you can't, you can't. When you think it's hard, it's hard."

"I know, you've told me this before, but it's hard to stay positive when the other team is so good."

"When the other team is so good, that's the most important time to stay positive. Let me give you a couple of phrases to say to keep your mind focused on a positive result. 'I look forward to rising to the challenge of today's game.' Or 'I play my best no matter what team we play.'"

Alberto's father has been down this road with him before. He knows that children don't always learn a concept the first time they hear it. He is prepared to go down the same road, teaching the same lesson as many times as is necessary to help Alberto learn about the power of words, the Attraction Principle, and the self-fulfilling prophecy.

Plant to Harvest

Most children understand how things grow in the natural world. They know about the planting/caregiving/harvest cycle of food. They have seen carrots, apples, and pumpkins go from seed to full grown. They know the story of the mighty oak that was once an acorn. Use that knowledge in your classroom or home to help children learn how thoughts can be planted, cared for, and harvested later.

One evening in late May the Nielson family sat around the kitchen table eating salsa from a jar.

"How do they make this stuff?" asked the youngest, age seven.

"It's made mostly from tomatoes, onions, peppers and spices," his mom replied.

"Can we make some sometime?" questioned the youngster.

"Sure, we can do it this summer," he was told.

The Neilson parents could have gone to the store, bought the necessary ingredients, and created a wonderful lesson on how to make salsa from fresh vegetables. They chose not to do that. Instead, they saw this as an opportunity to help their children learn a more valuable lesson, one that could help them see the similarities between seeds and thoughts.

The Nielsons decided to design a summer activity around the planting of tomato seeds. They started by talking with their children about the type of tomatoes they wanted to grow. Cherry tomatoes, pear tomatoes, or canning tomatoes were the choices. Big juicy tomatoes became the final selection.

They queried their children on what they wanted to do with the tomatoes once they were full grown. "Make salsa" was the first response. Make catsup, use them in salads, and fry them to perfection were other suggestions.

The next step took place at the local nursery, where the appropriate seeds were selected by the entire family. Then a growing area was established in the corner of the family room where the seeds could be placed under plant lights. It was determined that once the plants were large enough and the weather warm enough, a single plant would be selected and then transferred outside.

A growth chart was created along with a watering and an organic fertilizing schedule. Each family member had responsibilities to fulfill. Each week pictures were taken of the seeds and then the plant. The photos were then added to the tomato chart.

As the summer progressed, the family created a cookbook complete with photos of the dishes they planned to make when the tomatoes were harvested in the late summer.

What was most interesting about the tomato plant summer project was the discussion that took place one September evening as the family sat eating chips and homemade salsa.

Dad started the discussion. "As we sit here eating our homemade salsa, think back to the little tiny seeds we planted four months ago. Wow, we did a lot of work to help the plant grow just the way we wanted, and look what we have now."

*"We have even been giving tomatoes to the neighbors,"
added Mom. "What started with one little seed and
some special care from all of us has turned into tasty
food for us and others."*

*"What's so cool is that we created all of it from a single
idea. We thought about having our own salsa back in
May and created it in September by planting one seed,"
commented Dad.*

*Everyone took a moment to fill another chip with salsa
as they thought about the tomato seeds and the salsa
that resulted from the family's creative effort. Then
Dad continued, "We plant seeds every day when we
have an idea and then decide to make that idea real.
Everything you see around us started with a single
idea. Like a seed, someone took that idea and helped it
grow and get bigger. I wonder what other ideas the people in this family are going to create. I guess I'll just
have to wait and see what comes next."*

It was no accident that the Nielsons asked their children what they wanted as the end product. With that
information, they were then able to help their children
make the connection between the thoughts they had
(make our own salsa) and the end result (ripe tomatoes to use for salsa). Their children planted two different kinds of seeds (thoughts and tomatoes) and
each came to fruition.

Following are some commonly used expressions in
our society. Challenge your students/children to think
about them, write about them, and talk about them.
Where do these terms come from and what do we
mean by them?

- Seeds of depression
- Seeds of anger
- Seeds of frustration
- Seeds of harmony
- Seeds of war
- Seed capital
- Seeds of opportunity

What do you think about the material we have presented so far? Remember, the thoughts you think are planting seeds. Monitor your thoughts. Be sure you are planting what you want to harvest when you finish this book.

Attention

What you give your attention to increases. What you ignore decreases. Can you design lessons to help your children/students understand that process? Can you make that notion come alive in your home or classroom?

A mother in California read an idea in our book, Spirit Whisperers: Teachers Who Nourish a Child's Spirit, *and decided to adapt it for use with her family.*

"I want everyone to find an object in the room to focus on," she began as her family sat at the dinner table one night. "When I give the signal, I want you to give the object your full attention. I want you to concentrate on it for ten seconds. Okay, begin."

After ten seconds had elapsed, the mother said, "Stop. Now unfocus. Just let your mind wander without thinking of your object or anything else."

After a few seconds, she continued, "Now, focus on the object again, this time for twenty seconds. Give it your full attention. Bring your power of concentration to it."

When the twenty seconds were up, this mother said, "Okay, stop. Unfocus again. Relax your concentration." She paused for a moment. "Now make a spyglass with your hands." The mother demonstrated by making two fists, putting them together and then up to her right eye. She modeled the behavior she wanted from her children by looking through her fists at an object across the room. "Now, look at your object through your spyglass. Focus it by adjusting your hands back and forth. Focus on your object for twenty seconds. Bring it into sharp view with your spyglass."

When her children had completed her instructions, she said, "Okay, stop and put your spyglass down. Unfocus for a few seconds." After a brief pause she continued, "Now, use your power to focus again using binoculars." She made two "okay" signs with her hands and put them up to her eyes to demonstrate. Her children followed suit. "Now, look through your binoculars at your object. Concentrate on it again for a few seconds."

She repeated the process. "Once again, stop and unfocus. Relax. Let your mind wander." Then she gave further instructions. "This time I want you to put blinders on, the way we use blinders with horses to help them focus on what's in front of them and ignore distractions." Again she demonstrated by cupping her hands, holding them up to the sides of her face to sim-

ulate blinders. "With your blinders, focus on your object one last time. Begin."

"Okay, stop," she said a few seconds later. "Let me tell you why I asked you to do this activity. All of us have the power to focus or unfocus. We can all decide what to give our attention to and for how long to give it. We can use this power at any time," she assured her children. "It's called focused attention and it's within your power to turn it on or off. The main thing to remember is that it is you who is at the power switch."

"If you want something really badly in your life, you have to give it your full attention," she explained. Sometimes you may have to put your blinders on. Other times you may need binoculars. Regardless of how you do it, where you put your attention is your choice."

With that, this mother turned her attention to preparing dinner and her children scattered throughout the house.

The parent in this story gave her children an experiential lesson in focused attention. She helped them feel what it is like to concentrate, even though it was on a simple object somewhere across the room. They also learned what lack of concentration felt like. She had them turn their power on and off several times to help them appreciate that they operate the controls.

Contrast this with the parent who proudly proclaims his ability to multitask. This is the person who talks on the telephone, watches TV, and writes checks to pay bills at the same time. Often, these parents think they are helping their children by modeling the important skill of multitasking. Their belief is incorrect. They are teaching their children PFA, partially focused attention. This is not a helpful skill if you want to accomplish meaningful things in your life. Stop PFA in your home and school and teach your children and students how to focus their attention with intentionality and purpose.

Tim has high-functioning autism. He was diagnosed with Asperger's syndrome while he was in second grade.

Two things concerned his teachers as Tim moved through the grades: one, his antisocial behavior, and two, his fascination with birds. The teachers, staff, and administration found it difficult to work with Tim because all he talked about was birds. If a math problem did not include birds, Tim paid little attention to it. If a story was read that did not include birds, Tim appeared disinterested.

If you wanted to know anything about birds, Tim was the person to talk to. Even at the age of eight he had a vast knowledge about birds. Tim could tell you the eating habits, mating rituals, and migratory patterns for birds anywhere in the world.

The other students teased Tim and called him "the birdman," which didn't bother him because he loved birds so much and took it as a compliment.

A problem developed when the teachers thought it would be best for Tim to learn about other aspects of the world in addition to birds. He was forced to put his bird books away. He was disciplined when he refused to participate in classroom activities. He was recommended for special education classes because he wouldn't write his spelling words or complete his math assignments.

Completely frustrated with the approach the school system was taking with her son, Tim's mother decided to begin a home-schooling program. This was a difficult decision for her because she was a single parent who worked fifty hours per week to support her family. Yet, this parent felt something else needed to be done. What the school was doing was clearly not working.

Despite family and friends telling her otherwise, Tim's mother finally removed him from school in the fifth grade. Armed with current research on Asperger's syndrome, she decided to allow Tim's passion for birds to direct his learning. She would let him give his full attention to his passion.

Five years later, Tim is still "the birdman." And quite a birdman he is! Tim started his own business supplying local meat markets with organically raised chickens and fresh brown eggs. Because of Tim's successful business, his mom has been able to retire from her day job. She now works for Tim, delivering chickens and eggs to his customers. Not bad for a fifteen-year-old who likes birds.

What Tim's mother understood was that if someone else is controlling where you put your attention, you are giving them your power. By supporting her son in his desire to focus on birds, she helped him regain his personal power, concentrate on his passion, and block out all the extraneous material that was unimportant to him.

Buffer Zone

"Dad, I put a picture on my wall of the new bike I wanted and nothing has happened yet."

"I want a boyfriend. So where is he?"

"I've been thinking about getting a good job, but nothing has appeared yet."

The youngsters who made these comments do not realize one of the major premises of the Attraction Principle: that there is a time lapse between when you first think about something and when it shows up in your life.

This is good news if you are thinking negative thoughts. If your child or student is thinking he will never make the team, win first chair in band, or pass the test, there is still time to alter the outcome. Because of the time lapse, his thoughts, attention, and emotions can be changed to create different results.

The time lapse is bad news if you want what you want right now. If your child is filled with feelings of entitlement and thinks she deserves everything she wants right this minute, she will experience frustration.

We recently received an e-mail from a father who attended one of our workshops on teaching the Attraction Principle to children. He took our suggestion and shared The Secret DVD with his nine-year-old son. This is the conversation they had the day after viewing the DVD.

"Dad, I think that Law of Attraction stuff we watched yesterday is a joke."

"What do you mean, Robbie?"

"When I went to bed last night I wished for more Star Wars Legos just like that kid in the movie did with the bike. I got up this morning and there weren't any new Legos by my bed, like the DVD said there would be."

"So, you don't think the Attraction Principle works?"

"Right."

"One thing I've learned about the Attraction Principle is that there is a gap in time from when you think about something and when it actually appears. It doesn't always happen immediately. In fact, most of the time, it doesn't happen right away."

"So then it doesn't really work like they said."

"It does when you use the principle on a regular basis and in the right way. How about if we sit down tonight after school and create a plan on how to use the Attraction Principle to help you get more of the things you want?"

"I'm still not convinced it's going to work."

"That's okay. Like gravity or magnets, the Attraction Principle works whether you believe it or not. I'll tell you more about that part tonight."
"Okay."

To be continued . . .

Of course, this story isn't finished yet. A meeting will occur later that night, goals will be set, principles explained, and emotionality focused. Yet, this unfinished story illustrates one important concept: Children will misinterpret parts of what they learn about the Attraction Principle. In the same way they don't totally understand long division, a steam engine, or how birds fly, children will come to false conclusions, misdirected judgments, and inaccurate interpretations of the Attraction Principle.

See these mistakes and misinterpretations as opportunities to help your child or student learn more. Appreciate that they are involved in the material and processing it the best way they know how. That is exactly what each one of us is doing with this material: learning and growing in our individual ability to manifest our heart's desires.

What Is and Beyond

- *What is* is that there are no new Legos in your bedroom.

- *What is* is that you flunked the Spanish test.

- *What is* is that your sister keeps calling you disgusting names.

- *What is* is that you have two discipline warnings. One more and you will be assigned to the Responsibility Room for a day.

By focusing on the *what is* of their lives, our children

anchor that reality in place. If they continue to stay focused on *what is*, it will be difficult for them to change *what is*.

> "I have two detentions," Robert told his middle school counselor. "One more and I'm in R&R."

> "What's your goal for today?" Robert's counselor asked.

> "She'll give me another one if I even turn around."

> "What's your goal for today?"

> "She doesn't like me. I can feel it."

> "How would you like this day to end?"

> "I don't know."

> "Robert, would you like a suggestion?"

> "I guess."

> "Move your focus away from what you think is to how you want it to be. Concentrate on that for a while."

> "What do you mean?"

> "I mean that you're so focused on what you think is happening, you're neglecting to think about what you want to have happen."

> "But she is picking on me. Everyone else thinks so, too."

"And how is concentrating on that, thinking about it, and talking about it with your friends working for you?"

"Not too good, I guess."

"Then you might want to think about something else. I suggest you concentrate on how you want it to be."

"I'm not sure that will work."

"Well, you are sure how the other strategy is working, right?"

"Right."

"Well, think about it and I'll see you tomorrow."

"Okay."

The effort by Robert's counselor in this instance is to get Robert to move away from focusing on *what is.* The goal is to move him to a place where he sees and concentrates on *what could be.* What Robert doesn't know is that what his counselor is doing is exactly the same thing. He is focusing on *what Robert could be,* not on the way he is currently seen by some of his teachers.

Examples of useful Parent/Teacher Talk to get children to focus on the end result are:

- "When you're finished, what do you want it to look like?"
- "What is the effect you want your art work to have?"

- "What emotion are you trying to create in people with this story?"
- "What do you want your tower to look like?"
- "What taste do you want to create with the meal?"
- "How do you want the car to look when you are done washing it?"

Margaret was in the process of remodeling her seven-year-old's room when she had an idea. She could use this project to lay the groundwork of an important concept in the Attraction Principle: to think from the end first.

Margaret's original plan was to paint a mural of a meadow filled with Madison's favorite flowers and butterflies on the wall of her daughter's bedroom. She was going to take a day off from work and surprise her daughter with the finished bedroom when Madison returned home from school. But once Margaret decided to seize the opportunity to teach about the Attraction Principle, she changed her plans and involved her daughter from the beginning.

Mother and daughter began by looking at the wall and the way it currently was. They were in agreement that a change was needed. Now the task was to move the child from focusing on the way it presently was to how she wanted it to be.

The mother/daughter team searched for pictures of meadows and fields of wildflowers to get an idea of what the child wanted the wall to look like when it was finished. They searched through several books and magazines until they found the perfect picture that showed exactly what Madison wanted. Once they had a clear picture of what the wall was going to look like at the end of the project, they headed to the store to pur-chase the paint.

The following day, Mom took a day off from work and Madison stayed home from school. Together they trans-ferred the picture in the magazine to the wall, creating a full-size mural of a wildflower meadow in full bloom.

Was it worth this child missing a day of school to com-plete this project? The bonding that occurred, along with lessons on planning, purchasing, painting and cleaning up, should be enough to answer that ques-tion. If not, then throw in the feelings of satisfaction that come from accomplishing an important goal.

Although all the lessons listed above are important, they pale in comparison to the value received from the experience of starting from the end first. By starting from the end first, this mother helped her child raise her vision from *what is* to *what could be.* With that vision in mind and a picture of it to guide them, they were able to make it happen, all in less than a day. We hope they take a day off more often.

"As you know from yesterday, many of you didn't do well on the history test," Mr. Conner told his high school students. "We didn't do well as a class, either. Many of you were disappointed. I was disappointed. And some of your parents were probably disappoint-ed."

"Yesterday we spent the entire hour going over the answers and examining your responses in detail. We spent a lot of time talking about what is. Hopefully, many of you learned where and perhaps why you did-

n't do so well."

"Today we're going to do something different," he continued. "Please take out your journals and turn to the next clean page. Put your test score in the middle of the page and circle it. When I give the signal I want you to use that same page and write for five minutes. Write about your feelings concerning your grade, what you learned, what you attribute your grade to, and what you could have done differently. Okay, begin."

Mr. Conner called time exactly five minutes later. "Now," he said, "take hold of the upper right-hand corner of your page. Everybody have a hold on it? On the count of three, turn it. One, two, three."

"What do you see?" he asked after everyone had done as instructed. His students, unsure of what the right answer might be, responded with only blank stares.

"What do you see?" he asked again.

"A blank page," someone finally said.

"Nothing" and "An empty piece of paper" were the tentative responses offered by two more students.

"Exactly," the teacher said. "There is nothing there. You have a clean slate. You have just turned the page on your first history test of the semester. Think of turning the page as leaving the past behind. There is nothing you can do about the what is of that grade."

"Now it's time for us to move forward. On the blank page, put the grade you want on the next test in the middle and circle it. Then list several comments you *want me to write on your paper. Create the vision of what you want in the future. If you can imagine it, if you can articulate it, it can happen.*

"Your homework assignment for tonight is to make me a copy of the page you just completed. That way we can each have a copy of your vision. See you tomorrow."

Adapted from *Spirit Whisperers: Teachers Who Nourish a Child's Spirit,* by Chick Moorman, Personal Power Press, www.personalpower-press.com.

Teaching the Attraction Principle to students is not something you do on Friday afternoon or for half an hour during third period. It is something that can be infused into whatever subject you teach. In this case, Mr. Conner delivered the lesson simultaneously with lessons in history.

Reframing

Sometimes children get so locked into seeing things one way it is helpful for them to learn the skill of reframing.

- Losing the big game can be seen as awful or can be reframed to be the catalyst that starts us on a seven-game winning streak and a trip to the play-offs.

- Breaking up with your boyfriend can be terrible or an opportunity to play the field.

- Having a friend who confronts you about your behavior could be seen as an act of caring.

- Having classmates tease you about your clothes could be a blessing in that it helps you learn who your friends really are.

"I hate Juan," seven-year-old Pablo announced at the dinner table. "He's so stubborn."

"I thought he was your best friend," countered Pablo's mother.

"Not anymore. I've never seen anyone so thickheaded."

"I wonder if there isn't another way to see that," his mother remarked.

"What do you mean?"

"I mean, what if you saw 'stubborn' through a different set of glasses?"

"Huh?"

"Like when you put on sunglasses or 3-D glasses everything looks different. Sometimes when you see things through different frames they don't look the same."

"Mom, you're not making sense. Give me an example."

"What if you were wearing your 'friend' glasses or your 'he's on my side' glasses? What if Juan stubbornly stood up for you in an argument? What if he was

using that same stubborn attitude in that situation? How would stubborn look then?"

"Then it wouldn't be so bad, I guess."

"What if he wanted to finish something and stubbornly worked on it until he completed it? Maybe 'stubborn' could be seen as 'determined' in that situation."

"I guess. Have we got extra pie tonight?"

"Why?"

"I thought I'd call Juan and see if he wants to come over."

"Yes, we have plenty, unless he stubbornly eats the whole thing!"

"Oh, Mom!"

Pablo's mom did not set out to teach about reframing. But because she stayed conscious she was able to use the situation that the universe presented to her to help her son get in touch with an important point.

Will Pablo and Juan be best of friends forever now? Maybe. Maybe not. What is likely is that they will present this mother with many more opportunities to teach valuable life lessons.

Solution Seeking

Think about a problem and you send out negative vibrations. Criticize, worry, condemn, and you send out negative vibrations. Complain about a situation and negative vibrations again fill the air.

Teenagers complain. Young children complain. Preteens complain. In fact, once children get old enough to talk, they complain.

Children worry, criticize, condemn, and think about problems. And when they do, negative vibrations go out into the universe. One important strategy for helping your children or students turn those negative vibrations into positive ones is to help them learn to seek solutions.

Here are some examples of Parent/Teacher Talk that helps children move their focus to the search for solutions.

- "How can you and your sister both get what you want?"
- "Who would be willing to help me search for solutions on this?"
- "Sounds like you have a problem. What have you thought of so far?"
- "What ideas have you come up with for solving that?"
- "What possibilities exist for finding a solution?"
- "Sounds like you need to switch to a search for solutions. Can I help?"

This kind of language can break the negative snarl that children get into when they hold too tightly to the problem. It catches their attention and frees them to look at the situation from a new perspective - one of solution seeking.

Matt Sundeen was a first-year teacher in Alabama. When his students returned from recess on hot days, he noticed much pushing and shoving around the drinking fountain. It seemed that many of his fifth-graders wanted to be first in line to get a drink.

Students complained when they got shoved. They complained when the person in front took too long. They complained when friends gave friends cuts. They complained there wasn't enough time for everyone to get drinks in the time allotted.

Matt decided to take action. "We have a problem," he said, following one more incident of pushing, shoving, and complaining. "I hear lots of complaining about the drinking fountain procedure. I think it's time to find a solution. Do you agree?"

"Yes," came the unanimous response.

"Let me tell you what it looks like from my perspective," Matt began. "In a minute you will get a chance to share your views. I see pushing and shoving and I hear lots of complaining and whining about the procedure. From my perspective it looks dangerous.

Someone could get hurt. Now, how do you see it?"

Several students spoke up, voicing their concerns, which included safety, fairness, time constraints, people who drank too long, and favoritism.

"Looks like we have a problem all right. Let me put it on the board here so you can all see it." The teacher wrote, "We need a way that everyone can get a drink in a timely, safe, and fair manner." Students agreed that

the statement captured the essence of the problem.

"Here's what we're going to do," this rookie teacher explained. "Let's focus on finding solutions and brainstorm possibilities for solving this situation. We won't take the time to rate or judge answers. We'll just list all the possibilities. Later, when we have a big list, we'll see if there are some items that can help us reach a solution. When we arrive at consensus about possible solutions, we'll put the suggestions into practice for a few days and see how it works. Later we can come back together and see if we need to make any adjustments."

The students agreed and the process unfolded with much positive energy and an eager desire to solve the problem.

You may be wondering what specific solution this class came up with. Their solution is irrelevant. What is important is the process, not the product that it produced. Matt Sundeen led his students through a solution-seeking process as much so they would learn the process as to come up with a meaningful solution. In doing so, he showed them how searching for solutions diminishes negative thoughts, energy, and emotion and switches the focus to thoughts, energy, and emotions that send positive vibrations reverberating through the classroom and on into the universe.

Taking Control

Many children and students do not realize that they create their own reality. That's not so hard to believe when you realize that many adults aren't aware of that fact either. Not being exposed to these concepts, youngsters just don't see the connection between thoughts, emotions, and what they manifest in their lives. Since they haven't been shown how to work the controls, they lose power in their lives and aren't as response-able as they could be.

Chick felt out of control and unempowered when he first started riding horses. He didn't know the cause and effect mechanisms of the four-legged creatures he had come to admire. So he took lessons from a local instructor, Leesa Massman. He expected to learn a lot about horses. He learned much more.

Leesa Massman doesn't teach algebra, social studies, or penmanship. She fills out no lesson plans, she has no scheduled bus duty, and she spends no time in the classroom. Yet Leesa is most certainly an educator in every sense of the word.

Leesa teaches children, young and old, to ride horses. She is not a professional educator. She has had no formal training in teaching. She knows horses and she knows children. And she knows how to affect the spirit in each.

The first time I observed Leesa giving a lesson to a young child, the horse stopped abruptly and the child slid off. Leesa seized the moment and went with what had been presented to her as a teacher.

"Ball up and roll," she told the startled youngster.

"Roll with the punches. If you're going to ride horses, you're going to fall off. It goes with the territory. Even the most experienced riders fall off once in a while. Roll

with the punches. Don't fight it or resist it. Just go with it. And get back on right away. That's what we do in life and that's what we do with horses." The child got back on and the session continued even though the main lesson had already been delivered.

During another session I watched Leesa work with a youngster whose horse was making the mistake of taking off on the wrong foot when he switched gears to a faster speed. The rider was upset with herself for not cueing the horse correctly and was becoming frustrated. "What makes a good rider," Leesa told the concerned student, "is knowing how to fix errors. All students and all horses make errors. The trick is in knowing how to fix them. The only way to know how to fix things is to make a lot of errors. Then you get good at fixing."

The rest of the lesson was spent on making errors on purpose and fixing them. When the child or the horse made an error, Leesa had the student and the horse exaggerate it. "Notice how it feels so you'll recognize it if it happens in the show ring or when you're practicing on your own," she challenged. "Now let's work on fixing it."

During subsequent lessons I heard the following remarks as Leesa helped her students ride horses and learn valuable life lessons.

"Think confidently. If the horse senses your uncertainty, he'll take advantage of you. If you're not confident, it's okay. Just act as if you are."

"I like a horse that presents a mental challenge, because they make me think. Your horse is good that way. He is

making you think. He is making you a better rider. Appreciate him for that."

"She just did something smart horses will do. She distracted you from doing something you wanted to do. If she does anything evasive, put her right back on track. Your job is to stay focused on what you want to do."

"Here's your homework assignment. This week, as you ride, figure out what the problem is. You can't solve a problem until you know what it is. Then concentrate on solution seeking. Remember, the same method doesn't work for every horse. If it's getting worse, what you are doing is not helping. If it's getting better, keep doing what you have been doing."

"Appreciate your horse's problems. It's like working with an engine. If you only work with new engines that work effectively, you'll never learn how to fix engines."

"Nothing gets solved immediately. It might take a few rounds."

"The more you force, the harder they fight."

"If you're inconsistent, that's when they get resistant."

"Your horse can't beat you if you never run out of options. Act like you are in control and that you know what you are doing."

"The horse will take on your attitude, whether you are depressed or full of energy. Become an actress. Pretend like you have a positive attitude."

The lessons Leesa teaches have to do with more than just horses. They are lessons about life, attitude, energy, perception, persistence, personal power, confidence, self-responsibility, and control. Her vehicle is horses. Her destination is a child's spirit.

Parent/Teacher Talk that helps children take control includes:

- "How are you choosing to think about that right now?"
- "What thoughts did you decide to use to create that?"
- "What is a different way to think about that?"
- "Are you taking the thoughts that just came to you or picking one on purpose?"
- "Did you decide to think of it that way or is that how your friends thought about it?"
- "Are you thinking like a problem solver or like a problem keeper?"
- "What are all the ways we could choose to think about rain?"
- "What would you have to do to feel positive emotion about this?"
- "Can you re-mind yourself using what you've been learning about the Attraction Principle?"
- "Are you being the little engine that could or a different engine?"

Do you remember the boy in an earlier story who was upset when his Legos didn't appear the day after he thought he wanted some? Maybe you forgot. But his dad didn't. As promised, he met with his son later the same night.

After supper Robbie and his dad convened in Robbie's

bedroom. His dad was carrying a big dictionary as he walked into the room. Without saying a word, he dropped it on the floor, creating a loud thud. Robbie saw it happening and still jumped slightly when the book hit the ground.

"Why'd you do that, Dad?"

"I'll explain in a moment." His father bent down and picked up the dictionary. "This time close your eyes. I'm going to drop the book again, except this time you won't know I did it until it actually hits the ground."

Robbie closed his eyes and waited. The thud wasn't any louder than before, but Robbie jumped higher when the book hit the ground. "Okay, Dad, what's the point?" he asked.

"First, did you have any doubt that the book would fall to the floor, even when you had your eyes closed?"

"No," replied Robbie. "If you let it go, it will fall no matter what."

"The same is true about the Attraction Principle," Robbie's father said. "Your thoughts draw to you what you are thinking, no matter what." He paused a moment and then continued. "Second, when your eyes were closed, did you know the book was falling?"

"Not until it hit the ground."

"The same is true about the Attraction Principle. Sometimes you won't see what is coming to you until it's already present in your life. As I said this morning, there is a time delay. What you are drawing to you *could be 99 percent complete and you wouldn't know it yet. The dictionary was one inch from the ground and you didn't know how close it was to the ground."*

"Yeah, so how long is it going to take me to get the Legos I want?"

"Let's find out," replied his dad as he reached for his son's Lego magazine. "There are three basic steps in the Attraction Principle. Step one has to do with how you are being."

"What do you mean?"

*"**Being** has to do with how you are thinking and feeling about what you are drawing to you. This morning you were thinking and feeling that this can't happen. Let's change how you are being toward having the Legos you want."*

He paused and looked around his son's room. "Pick three Star Wars structures from this magazine that you would like to have. Then cut out the pictures, glue them to a piece of paper, and put the paper on your nightstand next to your bed. Every night before falling asleep and every morning before getting out of bed, look at your pictures. Think about having those Lego structures and say to yourself, 'The Lego pieces I want will come to me when the time is right.'"

Robbie gave his father a puzzled look. Dad continued, "Go ahead and cut out the pictures now and I'll tell you the next step."

When Robbie had finished, his dad continued, "The second step is to do something toward getting what you want. What are some things you could do to get one of the Lego structures you want?"

Robbie thought for a moment. "I suppose I could buy one myself," he said, then quickly added, "but I don't have enough money."

"Let's just come up with a bunch of things you can do first, without eliminating any. What else could you do?"

"I could ask you to buy me one."

"Keep going, what else?"

"I could ask Gramma. She's always sending me something from Arizona."

"Okay, that's three. Do you want to come up with more?"

"No, I want to do a couple of these."

"How about this?" interjected Dad. "Count the money in your piggy bank and see how much you have."

Robbie interrupted, "I have eighteen dollars and seventy-three cents."

"Good," replied Dad, pointing to one of the Lego structures in the catalog. "This one here is twenty-four ninety-five. If you wash and vacuum my car and your Mom's car, I'll give you the rest of the money to buy it." He paused. "Perhaps you could call your Gramma and talk to her about getting you one of the other ones for your birthday or for Christmas."

"Okay, I can do your car tomorrow after school and Mom's the next day. I'm going to give Gramma a call."

Legos and horses at first glance may seem like unlikely objects with which to learn lessons about the Attraction Principle. Actually, any object or situation lends itself to teaching these important life lessons. Remember, all that is required is a desire to do it, making the commitment, and following through with your parenting or teaching time and energy.

Six weeks later a box arrived with a note attached: "I thought you might not want to wait until your birthday. Love, Gramma."

Robbie's Dad smiled and said, "I didn't even know she was going to do that, did you?"

"No," answered the happy boy.

"Imagine that," his father said. "That package was sent all the way from Arizona. It was almost here and you never saw it coming. I wonder what else is coming your way that you don't see yet?"

Nothing more was said that day as Robbie raced off to his bedroom to put together his latest acquisition.

Focusing on Lack

Many of us have asked children, "Are you seeing the glass half full or half empty?" Usually that question is asked when a child or student is being pessimistic.

The half full/half empty analogy is rarely used when optimism reigns. Isn't that interesting? Does that mean we are more likely to notice and mention the negative, too? Could be.

When children focus on lack, it is often revealed in their language. When that occurs, gently guide them to new language by asking them to rephrase their statement.

When a child says, "I'm not going to cuss anymore," he is focusing on the negative. He is talking about what he won't do. That expression takes many forms.

"I won't hit him again."
"I won't be late for class."
"I won't use those words."
"I won't make a mess."

When you hear versions of "I won't" or "I'm not going to," reply inquisitively, "What *are* you going to do?" That question asks your child/student to switch the focus from lack (negative phrasing) to the desired result (positive phrasing).

"I won't hit him again" then becomes, "I will tell him in words when I'm angry."

"I will be here on time" replaces the negatively phrased, "I won't be late for class."

This type of language exercise gets your students or children speaking and thinking about what will happen when the appropriate result is in place. It is a way of thinking and speaking that will become a positive habit when practiced regularly.

Trinity came bustling in the back door three minutes after she had left to catch the school bus.

"I forgot my book bag," she stated.

"Looks to me like you just remembered your book bag," her mother told her.

"Yes," Trinity repeated. "I just remembered my book bag."

There is a big difference between "I forgot my book bag" and "I just remembered my book bag." Talk one way and you see yourself as a forgetter. Talk the other way and you see yourself as a person who remembers. How do you want your children to see themselves?

Help youngsters use words that express sufficiency and it begins to change their focus.

"I don't have enough time" can be changed to, "I have just enough time to get this part completed."

"I could only find three sources for my paper" can be stated, "I was able to find three useful sources for my paper."

Teach your children to speak the truth.

"There is no food in the house" is not true. "There is plenty of food in the house, and I chose not to eat any that we have" is true.

"I never get to do what I want" is not true. "Sometimes I get to do what I want and other times I have different choices" is true.

When children think about what they want and then focus on the fact that they don't have it yet, they are delaying the process. They are hindering themselves. Help them to focus on receiving what they want by noticing evidence.

Look for Evidence

One of our jobs as teachers and parents is to help our children notice proof. Find proof that your dreams are becoming reality and those dreams appear more possible. Even the tiniest clue can bring hope and increased expectation that more is on the way. Belief and expectation are strengthened when proof arrives.

"You improved your grade on this paper, Miguel. You're on the way to your goal."

"Did you see those girls looking at you in the mall? That's proof that the one you want is getting closer."

"You kept that bike going for ten seconds. You're almost there."

Richard was walking with his nine-year-old son, Jacob, to the corner store to buy a couple of fountain drinks when he spotted a penny on the ground.

"Hey, look, my son. I found a penny."

"Yeah, so it's just a penny. Pennies don't mean much."

Richard stopped, picked up the penny, and said, "They

mean something to me. They mean that money is still coming my way and all I have to do is notice where it is."

"It's still only a penny, Dad. Get real. You can't buy anything with a penny these days."

"Maybe not. But it's a sign to me that more is on the way and that money comes to me in unexpected ways. When I find this kind of proof, no matter how small, I appreciate it. That's what keeps more coming to me."

"Whatever."

At this point in his life, Jacob is skeptical and appears uninterested in the Attraction Principle. Notice that the skepticism does not faze the parent. This father keeps right on modeling the message he wants his child to learn. He knows that attitudes are often more easily caught than taught. He also suspects it may take several repetitions of this lesson before his son finds the value of it in his own life.

Emotional Feedback

As adults, it is often easier for us to use our emotional guidance system than it is for our children to use theirs. That's because we have a more highly developed feeling vocabulary and are more in tune with our feelings and what those feelings mean. We've had a lot more practice at experiencing feelings and dealing with them than our children or students have.

Upon seeing the signal that outdoor playtime was over,

four-year-old Erin flopped on the ground and began screaming. A temper tantrum on the preschool play-ground had just begun.

Mrs. Pendleton, a Montessori teacher for eighteen years, moved in quickly. She bent down next to Erin and said, "You sound angry. You didn't want to go in right now. You wanted to stay out longer and play in the sand. You're frustrated and your body is feeling anger. Do you feel the anger in your body? Can you feel how your hands are tight and your feet are kicking from the anger? Erin, can you feel it?"

Erin gave Mrs. Pendleton a quick glance and then began kicking the ground again.

Mrs. Pendleton immediately responded, "Erin, it's okay to feel your anger. Let's go inside where we can talk more about your feelings and how to tell others about those feelings."

The teacher took Erin's hand and helped her to her feet. "There, let's use those angry feet to stomp our way into the school and then we'll find other ways to let your anger out."

Together, the two stomped their way back to the school.

Once in the classroom, this veteran educator used the situation to design a spur-of-the-moment lesson on feelings. Each student was given an opportunity to draw pictures about feelings, make clay representations of feelings, and talk about being angry, sad, scared, or happy.

By helping children understand the names for feelings, this teacher laid the groundwork for building toward effective use of the emotional guidance system later on. Once children have names for their feelings, it is easier for them to notice them as they arise, accept them for what they are, not be frightened by them, and use them as important feedback.

Samantha was a seven-year-old bug fanatic. She loved to hunt for bugs in the dirt, discover spiders in their webs, and watch ants as they dragged a leaf across the sidewalk.

One evening while playing with her older brother, she spotted a huge spider in the middle of a new web on the bottom of the swing set. "Avery, come look at this spider," she called. A bug lover himself, Avery came running over immediately.

"Let's feed it and watch what happens," he suggested and raced off to find spider food. He found an ant on the sidewalk nearby. Seconds later he returned and tossed a black ant into the web.

Within seconds the spider zipped across the web, grabbed the ant, and began wrapping it tightly in its web. The ant suddenly became motionless as the spider stood over its prey. The entire ordeal took less than ten seconds.

As the two children stood quietly staring at the web, their father looked up from weeding the rock garden. Sensing emotion in their silence, he quickly moved across the yard to his children. "What's happening?" he asked.

"We fed the spider," said Samantha. "But I didn't like it."

"You look sad and surprised. Did something happen that you didn't expect?"

"Yeah, I thought it would be a good idea to feed the spider, but as soon as the ant stopped moving I thought that it wasn't a good idea for the ant."

"Yes, Samantha," her father acknowledged. At that moment you felt sad for the ant. Then the sadness surprised you because you didn't expect to feel that way. You felt sadness and surprise together. It's okay to feel sad and it's important to talk about your feelings so you can understand them better." He paused for a moment, looking at the sadness on both of his children's faces, then added, "Let's go sit on the porch swing for a few minutes and just let our feelings be what they are as we sit together."

Yes, children need help in understanding their feelings. Mixed messages about feelings abound in today's world. People often stuff their feelings and pretend they don't exist. At other times, they don't communicate clearly how they are feeling and sometimes send the opposite message. In order for children to use their emotional guidance system effectively, they need a better understanding of their feelings. Our job as adults is to help them develop that understanding.

The Distraction Principle

Sometimes children get so caught up in emotion that

they need to take a break and escape temporarily from the thoughts and emotions they are putting in their own way. That's when a strategic distraction is necessary.

At this time, children and students are so wrapped in negative thinking that they cannot purposefully distract themselves. That's where adults come in.

Ten-year-old Michael sat at the kitchen table poring over his math homework. Tears began to well up in his eyes as he became increasingly frustrated with the math problems. His father, Jerry, walked by and noticed his son's frustration. "What are you working on, Mike?" he inquired softly.

"A prime factorization tree," mumbled Michael.

"A what?" commented Jerry as he sat down next to his son. "I don't think I know what you're talking about. Show me."

Michael lowered his head and tears began to cascade down his face.

Jerry touched his son on the shoulder gently and said, "It seems to me that your brain needs a distraction, a little break from the math. Let's go outside and shoot some hoops together for a little while. Then you can explain this, uh, tree factor thing to me later."

While outside shooting baskets Jerry took the opportunity to briefly explain the Law of Attraction and the importance of distraction to his son. "Michael, sometimes when we think negatively about something we cause our brains to stay stuck on seeing only negative things. To change the negative thoughts, it sometimes helps to just go do something else. Doing something else helps our minds change the focus and let go of the negative. When we go do something that we feel good about, we can often get back to thinking positive thoughts. When we go back inside, let's hold onto the positive thoughts we're having out here shooting hoops."

After about twenty minutes Jerry said, "Let's head back inside and take a look at the math tree." As the two walked back to the kitchen, Jerry kept commenting on the basketball they had been playing. "You drained eight in a row from that one spot. That's your area. You seem to really be on fire from the left side of the basket. It looks like you've been out there practicing while I've been at work." His attempt was to keep Michael distracted from the negative thoughts about the math and keep him focused on the positive thoughts of being successful.

When they reached the kitchen table, Jerry said, "Show me this math factorization tree, and, remember, you know more about this than I do. So I'll need you to go slow with me as you explain it."

Michael sat down next to his dad. "Well, it goes like this . . ."

This is called a time-out. Do not confuse this with the time-out many parents use to punish children when they "misbehave." That practice is used by parents whose belief system supports punishment as a way to attain obedience and compliance. It is a misuse of the original time-out that was created for children who need a break, children who are in tantrum mode and need to quiet themselves emotionally and verbally. (See our special report, "Time Out for Time Out" at www.personalpowerpress.com.)

This time-out is intended for children who need to get away from a stressful situation. It is designed to give them a break so they can stop an onslaught of negativity.

If your children are in a situation where they are unable to get away physically, such as riding in the car or sitting in the classroom, teach them to get back to center through their breath. You can disrupt negative feelings and emotion and change your mental state with the power of breath.

"You're looking kind of stressed out today," Mary Weidenhawer told her second-graders. "I suspect some of you are thinking unhelpful thoughts. Let's stop thinking so hard for a minute and take a Big Breath Break."

"Take a deep breath. Breathe all the way down deep. Fill your tummy and your chest," she said, while demonstrating it herself. "Hold it. Now let it out slowly."

Mary repeated that simple process three more times. The brief time-out took only twenty seconds from start to finish. When the Big Breath Break was complete, she said, "Okay, let's turn our attention back to this morning's writing activity."

If a student or your own child is stressed or in a negative mental state, they can't always go outdoors, engage in a physical activity, or simply get up and move around. At those times they can change their breathing. They can make it slower, quieter, deeper, and steady. When they do that, they change both their thought process and their physiology.

A Big Breath Break infused twenty seconds of silence into the constant chatter, worry, concern, and self-talk that goes on in our children's minds. Give them an opportunity to get out of their minds and back into their bodies. Teach them to breathe.

Conscious Creation

"You guys talk like you believe children should be able to get whatever they want!" a workshop participant challenged us once. We can understand why she thought that, because we do believe children should be able to get whatever they want. In fact, we think it's our job to help them get it.

Helping kids figure out what they want is empowering for them. It gives them a picture of something to shoot for, a goal, a mission, and a passion. It gives them something they can work on attracting into their lives using all the valuable techniques presented in this book. It gives them an opportunity to practice using the Attraction Principle.

Helping children figure out what they want can be as simple as creating a Christmas list or back-to-school list with them. Helping your students create semester or weekly goals is also fairly easy to accomplish.

Forty-four hours. Friday from six p.m. until Sunday at

two p.m. That's the amount of time weekend parents have to make a difference, leave an imprint, and hopefully bump their children's lives in a healthy, helpful direction. Not much time. But, sometimes, time enough.

"I'm not going. Can't afford it," Buster Clark heard his daughter Jenny tell her best friend one Friday night, barely into his forty-four hours.

"Too bad," said the friend. "Lots of us are going."

"Where is this?" Buster asked, butting into the conversation.

"Germany," Jenny responded. "Most of the swim team is going."

"And you're not?"

"No. I'd have to try out, plus it's a lot of money. It costs a thousand dollars, Dad!"

Jenny's emphasis on the word "thousand" helped Buster realize just how big that amount appeared in her sixteen-year-old head. She could have easily substituted the word "million" for "thousand" and it wouldn't have affected the tone or intent of her comment.

Then the teens abruptly changed the subject, so Buster filed the Germany topic away under the category of "Things to bring up later."

"Later" came Saturday, when this weekend father caught Jenny alone in the kitchen. "Tell me about this Germany swim team situation," he said.

"It's with the YMCA," Jenny replied. "You have to try out. Most of the kids on my high school team are going to do it. If you make the Y-KATS, you get to go on the trip to Germany at the end of the summer. It's ten days.

I'm a good enough swimmer to make the team, but I'm not going to do it."

"Tell me more," the parent prompted her, sensing that it wasn't his turn yet and that she had more on her mind.

"What do you mean?"

"How did you arrive at your decision, and how are you feeling about it?"

"I decided not to go because it costs so much, and I'd never be able to get a thousand dollars in time. And I'm feeling left out because all my friends are going."

"So you're bummed because you'd like to be in on it and you don't see a way to pull it off?"

"Right. And I'll feel worse when they go," Jenny said.

"Do you want to go?" Buster asked.

"Yes!" Her answer was quick and decisive.

"Then why don't you?"

"Dad, I know you don't have the money. Neither does Mom. It's only four months away. I can't get a thousand dollars by then."

"Are you sure?"

"Dad, it's a thousand dollars. If I babysat every night from now until then I couldn't get a thousand dollars."

At this point, Buster realized that Jenny wasn't seeing herself the same way he was. His perception of her was of a persistent, determined sixteen-year-old who knew what she wanted and could figure out ways to get it. While it didn't matter to him whether or not Jenny chose to pursue this particular opportunity, it did matter that she perceived it as possible and herself as capable. So he pushed it.

"Jenny, there's no doubt in my mind that you can get that money together in time if you really want to go," he told his daughter.

"What?" she said. "What do you mean?"

"I'm saying I know you can do it."

"Do you really think so?"

"I'm sure of it. I know you, and once you set a goal and go after it, there's no stopping you. You always find a way to get what you want."

That slowed his daughter down. "Yeah. I am kinda like that, aren't I?"

Buster pressed the point home. "You sure are. So think about it some more, and we can talk later if you want."

"Okay," she said, and off she went to do the important things teenagers do on a Saturday.

If the story ends here, Buster could be satisfied. Jenny doesn't have to go to Germany if she doesn't want to. He'd probably be comfortable with whatever decision she made. If nothing else, at least he let his daughter know in clear terms that he saw her as a determined, able young woman. Anything in addition could be considered a bonus.

The bonus arrived on Sunday when Jenny informed her dad she wanted to talk.

"Do you really believe I can find a way to go?" she began.

"Of course," he said, without hesitation. "I've been thinking about the situation in the interim. I've decided I want to show you my support not only with encouragement and ideas, but also with a financial contribution."

"I don't think I can get the money," Jenny responded.

"Jenny," Buster said, "I want to help you pay for this trip if you really want to go. Here's what I'm willing to do. I'll match every dollar you earn for this trip. If you get five dollars babysitting, I'll match it. If you get ten dollars mowing grass, I'll give you another ten. If you get money as a gift for your birthday or Christmas, I won't match that. I'll match only the dollars you earn and save. I'm also willing to help you explore other ideas if that would be helpful."

Jenny took her dad up on both offers. Before she went home on Sunday night she had a long list of possible jobs as well as increased confidence and commitment to her goal of raising a thousand dollars. Her list included:

Babysitting
Lawn care
Laundry
Grocery shopping
Housecleaning
Tutoring
Catering
Car washing
Gardening
Reading aloud
Begging relatives

By the following weekend, Jenny had created and distributed a flyer to friends, relatives, and neighbors. no job too big or small, it proclaimed, and went on to inform people of her commitment, enthusiasm, and strengths as an employee. She explained her goal of going to Germany with the Y-KATS so that others would know her vision, and she asked for help.

That same week she wrote personal letters to all of her relatives telling them about her goal and plans and asking that any birthday or Christmas gifts be cash this one time only as a special favor and way of supporting her in something she cared about deeply.

When the calls came, Jenny responded. She babysat. She did lawn work. She baked cookies. She washed and folded clothes. She picked up black walnuts until her clothes and hands were equally black.

By the time she was finished, her efforts had cost Buster five hundred and sixteen dollars. His daughter made the Y-KAT team, went to Germany with money to spare, and had an unforgettable experience.

Buster combined several Attraction Principle techniques as he worked with his daughter on the Germany trip.

- He held high expectations for her and communicated that view.
- He helped her picture the end result.
- He helped her articulately state her want to herself and in her letter to others.
- He helped her focus on the solution.
- He helped her create a plan of action.
- He helped her eliminate doubt.

It is rare that one of the techniques presented in this book is used in isolation. As you help your own children or students learn these concepts, you will find yourself combining and blending many of the ideas to achieve the results you want.

Deciding what you want does not have to deal exclusively with obtaining material treasures. Nor does it have to be about wanting for yourself only.

The Hudson family maintained a charity jar that each family member contributed to every Sunday night when allowances were distributed. Each person, from oldest (Dad) to youngest (seven-year-old Sebastian), made regular contributions.

When the jar became nearly filled, the family would vote on where to send the charity money. In the past it had gone to save whales, support cancer research, and buy gloves for children in winter.

This year, when the jar was emptied and the money allocated, Mr. Hudson proposed a different plan. He had been reading The Secret *and* The Law of Attraction *and decided the charity jar could help him teach his children valuable lessons about wants.*

"Here is what I propose," he said, holding up the empty jar. "This year, let's decide ahead of time where we want the money to go. Let's be real clear what we want to do with it as we are collecting it. Let's keep that vision in mind as we watch the jar fill. What do you think?"

"I don't see the difference," one of his children offered.

"I'm learning that when you know what you want, when you're crystal clear about that, you attract it sooner. I'd like to experiment with that and see if it's true for us. Are you game?"

The thought of conducting an experiment of sorts appealed to the children, and after some discussion it was decided that they wanted to collect one hundred dollars to donate to a horse rescue ranch.

Wanting does not need to be exclusively for the benefit of oneself or one's family. Like the Hudsons, you can build a want list for the charity of your choice, your parents, your church, your community, or your favorite horse rescue ranch.

In your classroom you could create a desire to adopt a grandparent, write letters to servicemen or servicewomen, or rake the leaves of an elderly couple.

Why not get your family or students together and conduct an experiment?

Carmella's mother, Anita, was surprised to hear her teenage daughter ask to go to see a psychotherapist. She knew her daughter had been unhappy lately but didn't think it was that serious. Even more surprising was the fact that Carmella had a particular therapist in mind.

Concerned, Anita made the appointment and escorted her daughter to the first session. "I'm not sure why she asked to see you," Carmella's mother told the therapist. "She didn't tell me what it was about. I hope you can figure out what the problem is."

"I'll do what I can to help," the therapist reassured the anxious mother.

After Carmella's mother had left the room, the therapist initiated a conversation with her new patient.

"So, your mom tells me that you asked to see a therapist. What has led you to that request?"

"I listened to you on the radio and I heard you say that you teach people how to get what they want."

"That sounds like something I would have said. What is it you want that brings you in to see me?"

"Well, is it true that I can get whatever I want?"

"That depends on you."

"What do you mean?"

"First, let's talk about what you want and why you're really here."

"Okay, I want a car. I've had a driver's license for

almost a year and my parents won't let me get a car. I have to ask to borrow theirs, and most of the time they're using it for work or something. I want my own car."

"What kind of car do you want?"

"I don't know. I never gave it much thought."

"It seems to me that it's time to start thinking about it. In fact, it's time to start thinking about more than just a car. Let's start with an "at home" exercise. This week I want you to make a list of one hundred things you want and bring it back next week."

The following week Carmella returned with a list of one hundred and seven items. With the help of the therapist she separated the list into eight categories: career, finance, recreation, health, spiritual, personal, and philanthropy. The wants were then prioritized within each category and the top three in each category were placed on a separate sheet of paper.

"Let's work with this final list of your top three from each section," stated the therapist. "Pick a category."

Predictably, Carmella picked the category that had the car in it. The car was number one in that category. "I want to work on getting a car."

"What kind of car do you want?"

"I want a car that's reliable, dependable, and good on gas. It doesn't have to be brand new. It could be five or six years old and in good shape."

"Have you asked your parents for such a car?"

"Yes, but they say I don't need one and couldn't afford the gas anyway."

"They could be right about that. So your next step is to create the need, which means starting tomorrow you're on the hunt for a job. If you have a job you'll need a car."

The two then brainstormed several locations that were hiring and where Carmella was willing to work. A list was compiled and a plan of action decided upon. Before ending the session, the therapist added another "at home" exercise.

"Every night as you fall asleep, visualize yourself driving to school in your new car or going to your friend's house in your new car or coming out of work and driving it home. Do the same thing every morning just before getting out of bed. I want to see you back here in three weeks."

Three weeks later Carmella returned with a smile on her face. "I got a job two days ago. I'm working at a clothing store in the mall. I'm starting out working two nights a week and one day on the weekend." She paused. "My parents haven't said anything about a car. Are you sure this is going to work?"

"Carmella, let me explain something to you. The process of conscious creation can be ninety-nine percent complete before you actually see the results. Your car is already on its way."

"How long will I have to wait?"

"I don't know. What you can do is make the need big-

ger. Sometimes that draws a creation into appearance faster."

"How do I do that?"

"First, you continue doing the visualization we talked about last time you were here. Also, concentrate on giving your employer more than what they expect. Show up early. Stay a little late. Be willing to take someone else's place if they're sick or go on vacation. You'll probably get the opportunity to work more than just a couple of days per week."

"I don't see how that will get me a car."

"Let me explain. Over the next three or four weeks you will start working more, your hours will increase, or your employer will give you another day or two. Now think of this. Who will be taking you to and from work every day?"

"My mom or dad."

"They work and have schedules to keep, too. Four weeks from now, when you talk to them again about getting a car, you will have some money from your job for gas and to help with the insurance, and you will have created a need. After that discussion the car will be just around the corner."

Wouldn't it be nice if this story had a happy ending for Carmella? It did. Indeed, her parents were much more receptive to the car idea after they had driven her to work for six weeks. Shortly after that her father found the perfect car for Carmella, one that met all her initial criteria.

Carmella drove her new car home fourteen weeks after her first meeting with the therapist. During that time Carmella also worked with her therapist on prioritizing her want list and consciously creating the future of her choice.

Just prior to the publishing of this book, Carmella reported that she is now in her third year of studies at a leading fashion and design college in Europe. It is no coincidence that fashion design was the number one item in her career category.

Using Contrast

Children, like us, are good at figuring out what they don't want. Whether you are a teacher or a parent, you hear their negative desires often.

- "I don't like her talking about me behind my back."
- "I don't want to come home so early."
- "I don't want to have to read out loud in class."
- "I don't want to sit next to Jimmy."
- "I don't want to be in that class."
- "I don't want to go to bed so early."

Previously, we shared with you how to turn some of the "don't wants" around by asking, "What *do* you want?" Therein lies the silver lining of "don't wants." They are useful pieces of information that can be used to supply contrast and point children to what they *do* want. That's your job - to help kids take their "don't wants" and turn them into specifically stated and positively phrased desires.

"Mom, I don't want to go to bed," whined ten-year-old Ricardo.

"I'm sorry, Ricardo. I didn't understand what you said. Would you please repeat that in a normal tone so I can hear you better?"

"I said I don't want to go to bed."

"Thank you for repeating that. Now I understand what you don't want. That's a good starting point for helping us figure out what you do want. Let me finish getting your little brother off to bed and then we can sit down together and talk about what you do want and how to make that happen."

Twenty minutes later Mom called to Ricardo, who was reading a book in his bedroom, "I'm heading down stairs. I'll meet you at the kitchen table."

At the table, Mom opened the conversation. "Okay, from what I understand, you don't want to go to bed. I'm not sure what that really means. Do you mean that you never want to go to bed again?"

"No, I don't mean that. I just don't want to go to bed when Julio has to go to bed."

"Let's rephrase that into a statement of what you do want. It's easier to work on getting what you do want because you can create a clear picture of it. That way you focus on drawing it to you better. I don't know if you know this or not, but stating what you don't want

keeps your focus on what is not wanted. I suggest you consider changing your statement and saying what you do want."

"I want to stay up later than Julio."

"There, that's stating what you want very clearly. Now let's get it even more clear. How much later? One minute, five minutes, fifteen minutes?"

"Well, not one minute."

"If not one minute, then how many? Be more specific."

"I want to stay up one hour later than Julio. I'm ten and he's only six. I can handle staying up later than him."

"I agree that you can handle staying up later than your brother. I also agree that it's time for that to happen. And I prefer to build up to one hour. Let's start with a half hour first and see how you handle getting to sleep and getting up on time in the morning. We can do it for two weeks and then talk about how it's going before increasing the time to one hour."

"Okay, can I start tonight?"

"Yes."

Notice how quickly Ricardo's mom moved him through several stages of materializing his desire. First, he whined about what he didn't want. Second, she helped him communicate that without whining. Next, she helped him move to the third stage, where he stated what he did want. Fourth, she helped him become more precise about his desire. As a result, part of his want manifested right before his eyes. A lot of learning can happen in thirty minutes.

Revisiting Wants

- "I told my parents I wanted a new car and they got me one. I wouldn't be caught dead in it. It's embarrassing, just an old beater."

- "I know I said I wanted some dinner, but I didn't want this kind of dinner."

- "Yes, I wanted my schedule changed, but I didn't want Miss Gluster for my art instructor."

- "Thank you for renting me a movie, but this in not the kind I like."

- "I wanted ice cream, but not with chocolate on it."

The comments above were made by children who have an important lesson to learn about stating wants. They need to learn to get specific. Otherwise, they may manifest ice cream, but not plain vanilla. They may get their schedule changed, but lose their favorite teacher in the process.

Alexandro Gonzales disdained the drinking, partying aspect of celebrating New Year's Eve and chose instead to invest that important time in being with his children. A weekend parent who saw his three children only on regularly scheduled weekends and vacation periods, he valued every minute he spent with them.

Each year the Gonzalez children and their father would gather for the evening, munching on snacks, playing games, and enjoying each other's company. One ritual they implemented every year was that of goal setting. Each person would design a goal and share it with the rest of the family, telling why they chose that goal for the new year and what it would mean to them to accomplish it.

Alexandro took it as part of his parenting responsibility to encourage his children to make their goals specific. When his eight-year-old daughter announced she wanted to make a new friend in the coming year, he asked some clarifying questions.

"What kind of a friend do you want him or her to be?"

"Her," the young lady clarified quickly. "I want a her."

Other questions he asked included:

"What qualities do you want her to have?"
"How old would she be?"
"What kind of interests would she have?"
"Where would she live?"

The number of clarifying questions that were necessary during this activity varied with each child. Yet, when one was needed, Alexandro was willing and ready to ask it.

When it was his turn, Alexandro shared that during the coming year he wanted to publish a book.

His eight-year-old never hesitated. "What do you want it to be about?" she asked. "How many pages? Who do you want to read it?"

"Mission accomplished," Alexandro thought to himself, smiling.

One of the important reasons to teach this material to our children is so they can teach it to us when we forget. When you hear your students or children using these ideas on you, when you hear your own words coming back at you, pat yourself on the back. Give yourself some appreciation for teaching the concepts as well as for allowing your child or student to be the teacher.

Allowing

It is possible that our children or students develop clear wants, wrap them in positive emotions, hope for the best, and don't achieve the result they want. When that happens, chances are they need lessons on experiencing the state of allowing in their lives.

The state of allowing is characterized by the absence of doubt. Doubt is the primary preventer, keeping our desires away. You will know there is work to do on doubt when you hear comments similar to the ones below.

- "I can't do it."
- "I doubt if we'll beat that team."
- "I'm going to need a ton of luck on this test."
- "Yeah, she'd go out with me in a million years, maybe."
- "Our chances aren't good."
- "I'm wishing for the best, but I don't know."

- "I hope it works out."
- "I'm scared to get my paper back."

Students and children who talk like this are blocking their good from coming to them. They are defeating themselves with their words and their thought patterns.

Connie Warbler teaches language arts to middle school students in an old high school building in an inner city. She teaches them to match subjects to predicates, use proper nouns correctly, and know when to use capital letters. She also helps students punctuate, spell, and express themselves clearly. That's part of what is tested on the state assessment test that her students are required to take each year.

Connie doesn't stop there. "It's just as important that these young men and women learn the language of confidence as it is that they learn proper English," she often tells parents or anyone who will listen. "Just because the test makers don't think it's important enough to be on the tests doesn't mean it's not valuable. It fact, the language of confidence is more valuable than much of what we test for today," she adds, not exactly endearing herself to the school administration.

Recently, Connie gave her students a pop quiz to see if they could tell the difference between confident talk and talk that reveals doubt. These seventh-graders had no trouble placing her language examples in their proper category.

"This was an easy test," one of the students remarked. His classmates agreed. That's when Connie moved to

the next step.

"Now put an X in front of any sentence you have used or heard one of your friends use this semester," she directed. The discussion that followed the activity was lively and revealing. Almost every student had an X before seventy-five percent or more of the twenty-item list.

"We know this stuff," one of her students remarked, "we just don't do it. It's not how normal people talk."

Connie is helping her students get conscious. She is waking them up to how they talk and the effect it is having on their lives. She is giving them an opportunity to replace the language of doubt with the language of confidence.

The student who observed, "It's not how normal people talk," is correct. Normal people don't talk that way, think that way, or act that way. Connie, and many of you reading this book, are helping your students and children move beyond being normal. You know how and why to do that because you know about the Attraction Principle.

Want to gauge the state of allowing that is present in you children's lives? Ask them to write some "I want to" statements. Then have them add the word "but" and finish the sentence.

- I want to ride a two-wheeler, but my legs aren't long enough.

- I want a horse, but they're too expensive.

- I want a good grade in trigonometry, but it's the hardest class in school.

- I want to be Eddie's friend, but he doesn't like me.

"But" reveals doubt. It signals a blockage that is interfering with allowing.

"I can't" statements are a variation of blocking through doubt.

- I can't do it because it's too hard.

- I can't find another book on Santa Anna.

- I can't reach it.

- I can't concentrate with all this noise in here.

"I can't" statements are mostly untrue. They are examples of using language to limit oneself and simultaneously absolve all responsibility for the situation. Their utterance is evidence that the student or child has not internalized the belief that they create their own reality.

Challenge the limiting beliefs that surface when children use "but" and "I can't" by helping them write and speak allowing statements.

Allowing Statements

Lucy Matsui's daughter has cancer. Her hair is gone as the result of extensive chemotherapy and radiation treatments. The thirteen-year-old has spent six weeks being more than four hundred miles from her home and friends.

Lucy and her daughter, Myla, made the sojourn together, leaving three other children with their father. Since Lucy has read to her daughter every night since she was six months old, it was no surprise that she continued the practice in their motel room near the University of Michigan hospital.

The life story of Lance Armstrong and his courageous and inspirational battle with cancer was the first book they selected. In the evening they took turns reading pages to each other, learning about his medical experiences and his rise to the top of the cycling world.

"My daughter gets depressed sometimes and I use Lance Armstrong as an example of someone who beat the two percent odds they gave him of survival. That usually helps her feel better," Lucy reported. "The other night was particularly lonely so we took turns compiling a list of positive statements about cancer survivors."

This is the list Lucy and her daughter made:

Lots of people survive cancer.

There are millions of cancer survivors walking around right now.

Lots of girls my age have lost their hair and grown it back.

There is no form of cancer that someone has not

survived.

Lance Armstrong beat cancer and everyone else in the Tour de France.

Marquette is full of cancer survivors.

People are being diagnosed as cancer free this very minute.

Someone is walking out of the University of Michigan Hospital today, cancer free.

"Just repeating those statements seemed to help," Lucy said. "It lifted both our spirits."

What Lucy didn't realize is that she was constructing allowing statements with her daughter. The statements they created allowed them to challenge their limiting beliefs that cancer is awful and there isn't much hope.

Another way to help youngsters challenge their limiting beliefs is through the use of one- or two-word responses.

"Not true."

"For everyone?"

"Always?"

"Never?"

These short verbalizations are designed to get youngsters' attention and make them aware of their negative beliefs. Children need to be aware of their limiting beliefs before they can challenge their validity.

Child: "I always have trouble in math."
Adult: "Always?"

Child: "I can't do anything right."
Adult: "Not true."

Child: "I'd like to go, but the drive is boring."
Adult: "For everyone?"

Once your children or students become aware of their liming beliefs, you can help them move past them. Use of the word "yet" is a step in that direction.

"I'm not good at fractions" can be changed to, "I'm not good at fractions yet." "I'd like to go but I don't have enough money" can be rephrased as, "I'd like to go but I don't have enough money yet."

"Yet" adds a hint of possibility to the situation. The next step is to move children from "yet" to "It's on its way."

Help your students and children speak as if their desire is getting closer.

"If it's not here yet, it must be on its way."

"I'm not good at fractions yet, and I'm getting better."

"I'd like to go but I don't have enough money yet. And the amount I have today is more than I had last week."

Allowing statements help children see the desire as possible. Often it is helpful to have them think in third person. If they are focused on not having it themselves, guide them to think of others who do.

Sister Donna Marie takes her senior French students to Montreal every year as part of their foreign language learning experience. By immersing them in the language they learn more quickly as well as see another culture in action.

The students earn part of the money by having car washes, bake sales, raffles, and silent auctions. This past year, many of her students were being pessimistic about making the dollar goal the class had set for itself. Doubt was being openly expressed.

"I'm not sure we'll make it."
"What if we don't get enough money?"
"We're behind our midpoint goal."

Because it was hard for some students to believe they would make the goal and see themselves in Montreal, Sister Donna Marie switched their focus away from themselves to others.

"Do you think there is any French class in the world that went to Montreal this year?"

"Yes."

"How many?"

"Hundreds, probably."

"Do you think any of them went this week?"

"Yes."

"There is probably some French class getting on the bus right now to go to Montreal," one of her students chimed in with a hint of sarcasm.

"No doubt in my mind," Sister Donna Marie added.

"Let's compile a list of true statements about this," she suggested. The students agreed and offered suggestions which their teacher recorded on the chalk board. Ten minutes later they had compiled the following list.

Thousands of French classes go to Montreal every year.

Several French classes left for Montreal this week.

Some French classes probably left for Montreal today.

There is probably a French class leaving for Montreal this very moment.

Right now, a group of students from the USA is enjoying a meal in a French restaurant in Montreal.

Several students from the USA are probably walking down a street in Montreal right now with smiles on their faces.

An oral reading of the list followed its creation.

"I could see the cloud lift and the energy shift as we proceeded to read the list aloud," Sister Donna Marie

told us. "It was as if they could see it as possible again."

That's what allowing statements do. They allow you to see your desire as possible.

Positive Picturing

The universe doesn't care if your thought is real or imagined.

Bring an orange or lime into your classroom and cut it with a knife. What happens? You and your students will feel a sensation in your mouth. That sensation is called salivation.

Do the same thing without the real object present. Ask students to imagine a lime on their desk. Have them picture themselves cutting it open. What happens? The same salivation sensation kicks in.

The universe responds to pictures as well as to real objects. Therefore, the Attraction Principle works either way.

Vision boards are one way to encourage children to attract their desires using the technique of positive picturing. This can be as simple as putting a picture of the bicycle you want on the refrigerator or your bedroom wall. It could include the sophisticated construction of a corkboard elaborately decorated with pictures of one desire or divided into several different categories.

The process is simple. Still, it needs to be purposefully taught and demonstrated for children.

1. Decide what you want.
2. Find or draw pictorial representations of your desire. These must be pictures of your desire in its final state.
3. Look at your vision board regularly.
4. Add positive emotion to it. Feel the excitement of speeding down the street on that new bike. Feel the wind blowing your hair. Notice how happy you feel.
5. Do this on a regular basis and persist until the object or situation shows up in your life.

A vision board could take the form of a box or folder. It could be kept in your journal, book bag, or desk. We suggest the wall display when children are first learning this technique, as it is more visible and serves to keep the desire conscious.

Jean Claude and Danine make a deliberate effort to teach the Attraction Principle to their two children, Breanna and Jacque. Each child has a corkboard in their bedroom with a picture of themselves tacked in the middle.

Jacque's board is covered with pictures of Tae Kwon Do equipment he wants, a magazine picture of a golden retriever, books he likes to read, his third-grade teacher's smiling photograph, and a family vacation photo.

Breanna's board has her recent seventh-grade report card, a picture of the boy she likes at school, close-up photos of colorful flowers, a newspaper clipping of her gymnastic team's tournament win, a picture of the new hairstyle she wants, and a cutout of the cell phone she hopes to get for Christmas.

Both children look at their corkboard daily and add to it periodically.

Once a month, Jean Claude or Danine sit one-on-one with each child and talk about the pictures on their board and what each means. They discuss ways to take each thought represented in a picture and bring it to reality. Sometimes they talk about how a picture has shown up in their own lives and the feeling each has when a manifestation takes place.

Jean Claude and Danine know that teaching the Attraction Principle to their children is not enough. Although their commitment to teaching and demonstrating the vision board is important, please recognize that they have taken their teaching to a new level. They debrief on a regular basis.

Debriefing is a process whereby you give children an opportunity to think about and talk about their behaviors and choices and learn from them. In this process it is the parent's or teacher's job to invite children to think. By asking questions that require that children evaluate, analyze, prioritize, deduce, compare, contrast, and predict, we assure that we do not do their thinking for them. We help them to internalize the material at hand and make it their own.

Juan Hernandez arrived at the soccer field forty-five minutes prior to the game, as the coach had requested. This was Juan's first game starting in goal and his coach asked him to arrive early for a special coaching session.

When Juan approached the parking lot, he could see his high school coach standing in the middle of the field. Juan quickly grabbed his gear and hurried to meet the coach.

"Get all your gear on and then go stand in front of the net," instructed the coach.

Juan slipped on his gloves and jogged to the instructed position. He was ready for his coach to test him by kicking balls at the net and seeing how he responded. Juan was determined to show the coach that he had not made a poor choice in choosing him to be the netkeeper.

The coach did no such thing. In fact, he left all the balls sitting on the ground at midfield and walked slowly toward Juan.

"Close your eyes," he called. "I want you to see the field and all your teammates in position." Then he paused.

"Now watch the opposing team bring the ball toward you. See the ball clearly. See how slowly it moves. Everyone appears to be moving in slow motion except you. Focus on the ball. Watch as the ball is kicked on goal and you effortlessly snatch it from the air."

His coach was now standing directly in front of him. His voice was soft now. "Juan," he almost whispered, "take the next twenty minutes and envision different shots on goal like the one you just saw in your mind. You will see the ball clearly every time. You will stop every shot. Some you will reject. Others you will catch. Nothing gets past you. You are a wall in front of that net." He then touched Juan on the shoulder and walked away, leaving him standing alone in goal.

Juan stood there in the goal he would soon be defending, imaging the scenes his coach suggested. He felt strong and powerful, and he moved with quick, cat-like movements.

Twenty minutes later the coach walked back, touched Juan on the shoulder again, and said, "Now, go play today's game like you just saw it."

Mental rehearsal, creative imagery, and positive picturing are some of the names that have been used to describe this technique. It is a skill that great athletes and coaches use regularly.

Find stories of athletes and famous leaders who use positive picturing to help them achieve their dreams. Share them with your children or students.

Can you see yourself doing this with your children? If not, perhaps it's time for you to do some positive picturing.

Affirmations

It is possible to imprint your subconscious mind through repetitious thought. Using affirmations is one way to do that. Once an affirmation has made its impression on your subconscious mind, your old thought pattern will be replaced with the new affirmed thought.

Sally Constantine instigated a morning chant routine with her first-graders. After attendance was taken and lunch and milk counts recorded, the morning ritual begun.

"Are you ready?" she asked the class with much enthusiasm.

"Yes!" they responded in unison.

What followed was Sally chanting an affirmation to the class and the class chanting it back. Five affirmations were used in this process.

Sally chanted, "I am growing in my reading ability every day!"

And the class responded, "I am growing in my reading ability every day!"

Other affirmations Sally used were:

"I am increasing my math skills daily."

"I am becoming better and better at working with others."

"My listening skills are improving."

"I am learning how to take responsibility for myself."

Sally and the class chanted the same five affirmations for four weeks before she adjusted them by adding or dropping statements where she felt it necessary.

Notice that Sally did not have students chant, "I am good at math." The problem with that affirmation is that it is too easy to discount. Some students don't believe that statement at all. "I am increasing my math skills daily" is more believable. It is easier to find proof.

"My affirmation isn't working," Adrianna told her mother. "I'm not getting any better riding my horse."

"Tell me what you have been doing," her mother said.

"I wrote it on a file card and put it up on my tack space where I'll see it every day. I notice it every time I saddle Captain and every time I put the brush box away. And it isn't working. I'm still bouncing all over the place."

"What is your affirmation? Share it with me."

"Captain and I ride as one. We are in perfect flow and harmony."

"I see."

"And we don't ride as one. He goes one way and I go the other. It doesn't feel like harmony. I don't feel good about it. I don't even want to say it or read it anymore."

"Maybe you need to make an adjustment in your affirmation," Adrianna's mother offered. "I suggest you create one that sounds more true to you, one you can really believe for now."

"What do you mean?"

"How about something like this? 'Captain and I are

improving our flow and harmony. We are in the process of becoming one.'"

"Oh, I like that, Mom. I get a good feeling just listening to it. Don't forget that. I'm going to go get a pencil. Be right back."

An affirmation that is true for you will generate positive emotion. If negative emotion arises, an adjustment in the wording is needed until you can get that good feeling back.

Helpful sentence starters for affirmations that are more likely to be perceived as true include:

- I am in the process of creating . . .
- I am getting closer to . . .
- I have decided to . . .
- I am improving . . .

After Adrianna added the new affirmation to a file card and disappeared to do the things teenagers do on Saturday, her mother returned to her own affirmation journal. Already feeling deeply positive about the scene that had just unfolded with her daughter, she read again the affirmation she had been saying to herself for the past two weeks: "I am in the process of creating a close relationship with Adrianna." In reading it, she put into effect one important guideline about using affirmations: Use them after confirmation. A particularly strong affirmation is said or written immediately following a demonstration of proof. That's a time when your belief is strongest and your affirmation carries the most power.

Act As If

So your students are acting anxious about the test today. Challenge them to act as if they are confident. Think of it this way. The anxiousness they are revealing isn't who and what they really are. It's just their current act, one they didn't even choose, one they assumed out of habit, perhaps.

Pretending, playing like, and acting as if hastens the arrival of our desires. If your daughter wants friends, it is important to act friendly, to act as if she is a friend. Maybe she doesn't have a friend right now, but she can act as if she does.

Mary Sutherland teaches science to seventh-graders in a large suburban school district. Like many teachers around the world, Mary had attended one of our Teacher Talk seminars and heard us suggest that the participants add "act as if" to their Teacher Talk repertoire. We recommend that when students look up from their desks and whine, "I can't do it," or "I don't get it," teachers reply, "Act as if you can," "Pretend like you know how," or "Play like you are an expert."

While this strategy doesn't work with every student and it doesn't work every time, it does help many youngsters get off their "I can't" stance and take action. "Acting as if" gets students moving, gets them doing something. Helpful correction and direction by the teacher follows.

Over the past few years teachers have shared with us how they have used this strategy successfully with students who were working on long division, dividing fractions, and looking up material on the Internet.

Educators have reported success with six-year-olds tying shoes, sophomores demonstrating neck springs in physical education class, and a middle-schooler preparing to give a demonstration speech.

Although the application of this technique has been as varied and as personal as the teachers who have used it, no one has applied "act as if" in quite the same way as Mary Sutherland.

Mary's first-hour science class is her favorite. The students in that first-hour homeroom class are challenging and assertive. Mary enjoys both their energy and their spirit.

Most of Mary's first-hour students move on to social studies class during their second period. Occasionally, her first-hour students complain about second hour and their social studies teacher, saying, "She's boring," and "She doesn't seem like she enjoys teaching." One youngster asked, "Would you go talk to her and tell her to make class more interesting?"

During these times Mary simply listens and reflects the feelings and content of her students' comments without taking a position one way or the other. She listens as they vent and attempts neither to encourage nor discourage the remarks.

Mary has a third-hour planning period, which she often spends in the teachers' lounge enjoying coffee as she relaxes, plans, or corrects papers. Also having a third-hour planning time is Mrs. Millman, the social studies teacher about whom Mary's first-hour students frequently complain.

Guess what Mrs. Millman does during her planning period. That's right. She complains about her second-hour class. Mrs. Millman does not share the same degree of affection for these students as Mary has and she lets her opinion be known to anyone present in the teachers' lounge following second hour. "How do you stand them?" she once asked Mary. "They're so noisy and they can't concentrate for any length of time."

It didn't take Mary long to realize she was caught in a squeeze play. First hour she often heard from students how awful their second-hour teacher was, and third hour she frequently heard from the teacher how awful her second-hour students were. After a few days of this cross-venting, Mary realized she had to do something. She figured she had two choices. She could work with her students or she could work with the teacher. She chose the students.

"I took a workshop a couple of weeks ago," Mary explained to her first-hour class the next day. "The presenter told us about a strategy he called, ACT AS IF. He said that if you ACT AS IF you can, you can actually alter the way you look at the world and often change certain situations for the better." Mary gave a few examples and then monitored a lengthy discussion on the topic.

At the conclusion of the discussion, Mary challenged her students to use the strategy on Mrs. Millman during second hour. "What do you think would happen," she asked, "if you all went in there for two weeks and acted as if her class was the most interesting class you ever attended?"

The student responses came quickly.

"We couldn't do that."
"That's impossible."
"You don't know how boring it is in there."
"She'll never change!"

"It's just two weeks," Mary explained. "Maybe it won't make a difference, but at least we can check out this technique and see if it would work in this improbable case. How about doing it for just two weeks?"

The students resisted and Mary persisted. Eventually the students agreed to go along with the plan for two weeks as part of a science experiment. They would go to their second-hour class acting as if they loved it for ten school days, documenting both their individual reactions and behaviors and the teacher's.

Before they began, each student described in writing how he or she presently viewed the class, detailed the intervention he or she planned on making (acting as if they liked the class), and wrote a hypothesis concerning the experience and predicting the outcome. The "acting as if" strategy was discussed and role-played. Students decided that acting as if you liked a class meant you sat up straight, gave solid eye contact, smiled at the teacher, asked related questions, and participated during discussions. It also meant doing all homework assigned by the teacher.

At the end of the first week, students reported no change in their views of the class. The teacher seemed basically the same, and the class was still boring. Several students did mention, though, that they did better on the chapter test because they had been paying closer attention to the lecture and discussions.

During the second week, Mrs. Millman brought to school Chinese souvenirs and artifacts from her home. "My second-hour students seem to be behaving better," she told Mary during their Monday planning time. "I think I'll take a risk with them and do a couple of special things this week and see how it goes."

On Wednesday of the second week, Mrs. Millman brought in Chinese finger food she had prepared at home and some fortune cookies. The class asked related questions about the food and continued to act as if they were interested. Mrs. Millman noted the changed behavior and continued to mention it in the teachers' lounge.

At the end of the two-week trial period, students voted to extend the experiment for another week. "Mrs. Millman seems a lot nicer," one student offered. Many students agreed that the class was getting more interesting. The students reported that Mrs. Millman was smiling more in class and had stopped yelling.

At the end of the third week, the students turned in their individual science reports on ACT AS IF. All reported that the strategy helped change their social studies teacher's behavior.

In the staff lounge Mrs. Millman was heard to announce, "I've finally turned the corner with that second-hour class. It took me a while, but I finally got them where I want them."

To date, Mary Sutherland has not confessed her efforts with the science project to her colleague, Mrs. Millman. That's probably just as well.

By changing their own behavior, using an act, these students were able to influence the behavior of their least favorite teacher. Our children can unleash incredible power of manifesting. All they need is for us to teach them how.

The last week of school for teachers of students who are graduating in a few days is often difficult. "Senioritis" is the name given to the behavior of seniors who suffer from "who cares anymore?" disease.

You wouldn't know senioritis existed if you visited Mary Clayton's drama class the last week of school. Motivation is on the upswing. That's because the students are getting ready for their futures party.

Clothes have to be made, scripts written, story lines developed, and futures created.

On the last day of school every year, Mary throws a party for her students. She buys the soft drinks and chips and has sandwiches catered.

Students have been in preparation for a week or more. Their assignment was to imagine the life they want ten years from now. What would they be doing? Where would they be living? Would they be married? Would they have children?

On the day of the party, students will enter as if it was ten years later. This pretend reunion will last the entire class period. All conversation has to take place in the future.

As they enter the classroom this day, students begin to greet each other.

"Hey, Jimmy, how you been?"

"They call me James now. And I've been great. Jimmy wouldn't look too good on the door to my law practice."

"You're a lawyer? Wow. Congratulations. Maybe I should call you. I need to look at legal contracts for a new land deal I put together."

"What kind of land deal?"

"Super malls. I own six now and I'm looking to expand to another two."

"That sounds exciting. Here's my number. I'll be back in my Phoenix office in a week."

"You live in Phoenix now?"

"Yeah, I just moved back to the States from England. My wife missed her family too much so we came back."

"You got married?"

"Yeah, remember the cute girl in our chemistry class? Carlotta?"

"Sure do."

"Well, she's my wife now."

And so it goes for the entire hour.

The purpose of the futures party is multifaceted. It helps students create a vision of where they want to go, get specific about their plan, and act as if it has already happened. It infuses desires with credibility and shoots positive vibrations out into the universe.

Not sure you can design a lesson or use language that would help your child or student understand this concept?

Why not act as if you can?

Purposeful Anticipation

One of the greatest gifts you can give your children is your positive expectations of them. Children and students tend to live up or live down to our expectations, whatever they happen to be.

Another important gift we can give them is helping them develop the skill of expecting the best for themselves. If they wish they could go to an amusement park during the summer, they are not expecting it will happen. If they hope they make the team, they are not expecting they will in fact make it.

Wishing and hoping are a lot like sitting in a rocking chair on the front porch. It gives you something to do but doesn't get you anywhere. If a person sees you sitting there rocking on your front porch as they drive by and then they drive by an hour later, you will still be on the front porch, even though you rocked the entire time. The same holds true for wishing and hoping. Those vibrations keep you firmly planted in the same spot.

The following story was written for inclusion in this text by Reese Haller. Reese is Thomas's ten-year-old son. He is an author of four books and travels around the country sharing his eight steps of writing in a presentation entitled, "Catching the Writing Bug from One Kid to Another."

Last October I presented at an International Reading Association conference in Mobile, Alabama. Our hotel was about six blocks away from the place where I was presenting, which might not have been a problem if it hadn't rained the entire time I was there.

On the morning of my presentation it was raining the worst. I was all dressed up in my special suit and I had two big boxes of my Fred the Mouse books to sell. I was worried about getting to the place without getting all wet. My dad said not to worry because a car would come to pick us up.

We went down to the lobby to meet our car and the person at the counter said that our driver was in an accident and would not be able to pick us up. My dad asked the lady to call for a cab. Two women sitting in the lobby said they had asked for a cab thirty minutes ago and were told that none were available because of a strike. That's when I started to really worry.

My dad smiled and said, "A car will come." He does stuff like that when things don't look so good, so I wasn't surprised.

I went and sat next to the two women, who were teachers attending the conference. They said that they were worried because they thought they were going to miss my presentation. They said they were sorry that I was stuck with them and might not make it either.

My dad immediately interrupted and said, "A car will come." I had my doubts, but, like I said, that's how my dad is.

I kept talking to the ladies and my dad kept interrupting and saying, "A car will come." After about twenty-five minutes I got tired of listening to my dad say that and just sat quietly, worrying.

Then the front door to the hotel opened up and in walked a hotel worker ready to go to work. My dad ran to the door and quickly asked the woman how she had gotten there. She said that her husband drove her in because of the storms. Immediately, my dad ran out the door and returned a minute later followed by a great big man wearing his pajamas. My dad exclaimed, "My son, our car is here!"

The man in his PJs grabbed my boxes of books and out the door we went. We invited the two teachers to join us and we all squeezed into his little car. The man drove us to the event center, carried my books and my bag into the lecture hall, and helped me set out my presentation materials all while wearing his wet pajamas. I, on the other hand, was dry and on time.

My dad was right, a car came, and after learning more about the Attraction Principle, I realized that he brought it.

I think it is important for kids to understand that if you focus on something, negative or positive, those kinds of things will come to you. If you think hurtful things, hurtful things happen to you. If you think nice, pretty, bunny rabbit kinds of things, nice pretty things come to you.

You get what you think.

For more information on Reese's books and presentations visit www.reesehaller.com.

Action

Faith without works is dead. Children and students won't manifest much if they take no action. Yes, writing an affirmation is an action. So is creating a vision board. Identifying wants, looking for proof, and writing allowing statements are action.

These actions are critical because all the physical action in the world will not overcome negative thought and emotion, doubt, disbelief, and unsupportive vibrations.

When it is time for physical action, it is necessary to help our children and students take action that is meaningful. Meaningful action moves you in the direction of your desires.

Help your children learn they cannot do a goal. Goals are important. So are desires. Yet, you can't do them. For example, perhaps your one hundred forty-pound daughter has a goal/desire to weigh one hundred twenty pounds. To do that she has to lose twenty pounds. She can't just go do that goal today. What she can do today are activities that will move her closer to that goal.

GOAL: WEIGH 120 POUNDS

Activities:

1. Talk to a health care professional.
2. Buy a book on nutrition.
3. Read the first chapter.
4. Walk one mile after school.
5. Ask two friends to call me on Sunday and ask how I'm doing.
6. Pack my lunch instead of eating in the cafeteria.

Part of using the Attraction Principle is learning how to take the next step. If you are in high school, the next step to becoming an airline pilot is not jumping in an airplane and directing it down the runway. The next step might be investigating flight schools or service opportunities.

"What's your next move, Jarrett?"

"What do you think the next step is on the path?"

"If this were a staircase, what does the next level look like?"

"Billy, what would be a way to get started?"

The hardest part of anything is getting started. If children learn to make that first move with confidence, the universe will reward them with more information about what to do next.

Gratitude

"Those who have get more" is a saying you might have heard. A more accurate version from our perspective is, "Those who are grateful for what they have get more." Gratitude attracts.

If your daughter wants clothes and a pair of socks shows up in the mail, it behooves her to be grateful. If not, she could shut down the pipeline of supply.

It is no accident that Thomas was grateful for the man who showed up in pajamas to take him and Reese to the conference center. If he had thought, "This is terrible. I deserve better than this," cars would be less likely to show up in the future. The man who found the penny rejoiced because he knew that more was on the way. He was not being grateful as a technique. He was truly grateful.

"Mom, can we do the thank-you notes now? Please?" Those words came out of the mouth of six-year-old Ricardo Montero. It was only two days after Christmas and this youngster wanted to do thank-you notes.

A kid who likes to do thank-you notes? This doesn't compute. Have you ever met a child who likes to write thank-you notes? Well, Recardo does.

Valeria Montero has two children. Her son is six and her daughter is thirteen. Both enjoy doing thank-you notes. Here's why.

"I write thank-you notes myself," Valeria explains. "I make sure my children see me do it. I say things like, 'I'm going to write my thank-you notes now. It's fun for

me to let others know how much I appreciate their gifts." I'm careful to never, ever, let them hear me complain about having to share appreciation in writing.

"I send thank-you notes to my own children," she continues. "I pin them on their pillow, put them in their lunchbox, or send them in the mail. I did this even before they were old enough to read. When they asked me what it said, I read it to them."

Valeria is helping her children build the habit of gratitude. She is modeling the message and showing children through her behavior why appreciation is important.

Charity and the spirit of giving is another way of showing gratitude for what you have received. An important part of teaching children about gratitude is teaching the charity habit.

Many parents and educators used the destruction delivered by recent hurricanes and tsunamis as an opportunity to help children learn about charity and the importance of reaching out to others in their time of need. They have made generous family donations, often involving their children in picking out the charity, writing the check, and preparing and mailing the envelope. They have allowed their children to witness turning the pain and grief of unimaginable loss into a time for extending love and compassion to unknown people halfway around the world.

Clearly, disasters provide an opportune time to teach children about charity. But wouldn't you want lessons about charity to be more than a one-time occurrence?

What if you want the spirit of giving to be a way of life for your children? What if you want charity to become a habit?

The Radisons periodically go through their closets rooting out clothes they haven't worn in a while, clothes to be given to the Salvation Army or Goodwill for distribution to the needy.

They encourage their children to do the same. They allow them to select which clothes or toys they wish to donate. They get their children involved in choosing the appropriate items and take their children with them when they drop the items off at the charitable destination.

The value of this activity is diminished greatly if you go through your children's closets for them without their presence. Get them involved.

The Crandalls set up birthday parties as a time for giving to others. At their child's first school-age birthday party they asked guests to bring a gift of a book (new or used) to be donated to a local charity. They talked to their son about the books he had and about children who have no books. They explained that one way to celebrate a birthday would be to give to those who have less.

The Crandalls involved the birthday boy in the decision of whether to give the books to a women's shelter, a doctor's office, or some other appropriate organization.

When they delivered the books with their child, they recorded it on camera. Photos were posted on the refrigerator and later recycled into photo albums.

By implementing ideas like the ones above in your home or classroom you are teaching children that charity is not reserved only for emergencies. You are helping them appreciate that reaching out to others in need is a way of life rather than giving only when a catastrophic disaster occurs.

Remember, while you are giving to others, you are giving your children important messages about your beliefs concerning the spirit of giving, gratitude, and the Attraction Principle.

Conclusion

Your children are already skilled at attracting. Think of it this way. They took an important first step. They attracted you. Somehow, they brought you into their lives. They used the Attraction Principle to draw you to them so that you could teach them more. They know what they need and they know you are the one to guide them.

You, too, have taken an important step. You have attracted your children/students to you. You have brought them to you at a time when you have been learning much about the Attraction Principle. By now, you know this is not an accident or just some interesting coincidence.

You have also taken another step. You have attracted this book into your life. It didn't come to you out of the blue. You drew it to you using many of the processes explained on the previous pages.

So there you have it. You, your children, and the material contained in this book all coming together in the same place at the same moment in time. What an interesting triangle you, your children/students, and this book have become.

The secret of the Attraction Principle has been revealed to you, not by us but by those who have come before us. We have provided you with a glimpse of how to pass it on to others. Whether you're a teacher or a parent, you have been called. The children in your life have come to you so that you could give them the bonus lessons they desire.

You have been called to pass on the secret of the Attraction Principle. Why this is so is not important. Understanding how you created it this way requires no explanation, either.

The important answers belong with the following questions: Did you hear the call? Are you willing to take the next step? Will you recognize and use the teachable moments as they come into your life?

You are in the right place at the right time. So why not start right now, right here.

Take a moment to create an image of your children or students in your mind. Look at each child individually. Each one has come to you to learn a different aspect of the Attraction Principle. Some have come to relearn something they have temporarily forgotten.

You have come to teach. Or perhaps you, too, have come to recall something you have forgotten.

Regardless, you are now in the position to give a gift to your children/students that will change their lives forever. Are you willing to give that gift?

A B O U T   T H E   A U T H O R S

Portraits by Gregg

Thomas B. Haller,
MDiv, LMSW, ACSW, DST

Thomas Haller is the founder and director of Healing Minds Institute, a center devoted to empowering individuals with skills for creating interpersonal change, building relationship success, and raising responsible children.

He has maintained a private practice for over eighteen years in Bay City, Michigan, as a child, adolescent and couples therapist and an AASECT certified diplomate of sex therapy. Thomas is known locally as "The Love Doctor," appearing on a weekly morning radio program answering relationship and parenting questions on air.

As a widely sought-after national and international presenter, Thomas conducts full-day workshops and seminars for churches, school districts, parent groups, and counseling agencies. He is also a regular lecturer at universities across the country.

Thomas is available for the following topic areas:

FOR PARENTS

- *Teaching THE ATTRACTION PRINCIPLE to Children*
- *The 10 Commitments to Parenting with Purpose*
- *The Only Three Parenting Strategies You'll Ever Need*
- *How to Talk to Your Children about Sex*
- *How to Inspire Children to Write*
- *Managing Aggression and Anger in Children*

FOR COUPLES

- *The 7 Keys to Creating a Successful Relationship*
- *How to Talk to Your Partner about Sex*
- *The Language of Mutual Respect and Intimacy*
- *The 20 Best and 20 Worst Things to Say to Your Partner*
- *Success 101: How to Be Successful at Whatever You Do*

Want a customized workshop? Thomas will structure a workshop to meet your needs.

For more information about these programs or to discuss a possible training or speaking date, please contact:

Thomas Haller
Haller's Healing Minds, Inc.
5225 Three Mile Rd.
Bay City, MI 48706
Telephone: (989) 686-5356
Fax: (989) 643-5156
E-mail: thomas@thomashaller.com
Website: www.thomashaller.com

Portraits by Gregg

Chick Moorman

Chick Moorman is the director of the Institute for Personal Power, a consulting firm dedicated to providing high-quality professional development activities for educators and parents.

He is a former classroom teacher with over forty-five years of experience in the field of education. His mission is to help people experience a greater sense of personal power in their lives so they can in turn empower others.

Chick conducts full-day workshops and seminars for school districts and parent groups. He also delivers keynote addresses for local, state, and national conferences.

He is available for the following topic areas:

FOR EDUCATORS

- *Celebrate the Spirit Whisperers*
- *Motivating the Unmotivated*
- *Achievement Motivation and Behavior Management through Effective Teacher Talk*
- *Teaching Respect and Responsibility*

FOR PARENTS

- *Teaching THE ATTRACTION PRINCIPLE to Children*
- *Parent Talk: Words That Empower, Words That Wound*
- *Transformational Parenting*
- *Raising Response-Able Children*
- *The Only Three Parenting Strategies You'll Ever Need*
- *Parenting with Purpose*

If you would like more information about these programs or would like to discuss a possible training or speaking date, please contact:

Chick Moorman

P.O. Box 547
Merrill, MI 48637
Telephone: (877) 360-1477
Fax: (989) 643-5156
E-mail: ipp57@aol.com
Website: www.chickmoorman.com

BIBLIOGRAPHY

ATKINSON, WILLIAM WALTER. *Thought Vibration or the Law of Attraction in the Thought World.* Kessinger Publishing Company, 1988.

BESANT, ANNIE. *Thought Power.* Wheaton, IL: The Theosophical Publishing House, 1979.

BYRNE, RHONDA, *The Secret.* New York, NY: Atria Book/Beyond Words, 2006.

CANFIELD, JACK AND JANET SWITZER, *The Success Principles: How to Get from Where You Are to Where You Want to Be.* New York: Collins, 2005.

CANFIELD, JACK WITH D.D. WATKINS, *Jack Canfield's Keys to Living the Law of Attraction.* Deerfield Beach, FL: Health Communications, Inc., 2008.

CHOPRA, DEEPAK. *The Seven Spiritual Laws of Success: A Practical Guide to the Fulfillment of Your Dreams.* San Rafael, CA: Amber-Allen Publishing, 1994.

DAY, LAURA. *The Circle: How the Power of a Single Wish Can Change Your Life.* New York, NY: Penguin Putnam, Inc., 2001.

DELAFLOR, IVONNE. *The Positive Child: Through the Language of Love.* Lincoln, NE: iUniverse, Inc., 2004.

DYER, WAYNE. *Gifts From Eykis.* New York, NY: Simon and Schuster, 1983.

DYER, WAYNE. *The Power of Intention: Learning to Co-create Your World Your Way.* Carlsbad, CA: Hay House, Inc., 2004.

DYER, WAYNE. *Pulling Your Own Strings.* New York, NY: Thomas Y. Crowell Co., 1978.

DYER, WAYNE. *The Sky's the Limit.* New York, NY: Simon and Schuster, 1980.

DYER, WAYNE. *Your Erroneous Zones.* New York, NY: Avon Books, 1977.

DYER, WAYNE. *Your Sacred Self: Making the Decision to Be Free.* New York, NY: Harper Paperbacks, 1991.

DYER, WAYNE. *What Do You Really Want for Your Children?* New York, NY: Avon Books, 1981.

EMERY, GARY. *A New Beginning: How to Change Your Life Through Cognitive Therapy.* New York, NY: Simon and Schuster, 1981.

FABER, ADELE and ELAINE MAZLISH. *How to Talk So Kids Will Listen and Listen So Kids Will Talk.* New York, NY: Rawson, Wade Publishers, Inc., 1980.

FALCONE, VICKIE. *Buddha Never Raised Kids & Jesus Didn't Drive Carpool: Seven Principles for Parenting with Soul.* San Diego, CA: Jodere Group, Inc., 2003.

FETTIG, ART. *The Three Robots*. Battle Creek, MI: Growth Unlimited, 1981.

GAWAIN, SHAKTI. *Creative Visualization*. New York, NY: Bantam Books, 1982.

GILLIES, JERRY. *Money-Love*. New York, NY: Warner Books, 1978.

GILLIES, JERRY. *Psychological Immortality: Using Your Mind to Extend Your Life*. New York, NY: Richard Marek Publishers, 1981.

GINOTT, HAIM. *Teacher and Child*. New York, NY: The Macmillan Company, 1972.

HANSON, REBECCA. *Law of Attraction for Business*. Rebecca Hanson Publisher, 2004.

HICKS, JERRY and ESTHER HICKS. *Ask and It Is Given: Learning to Manifest Your Desire*. Hay House, Inc., 2005.

HICKS, JERRY and ESTHER HICKS. *The Law of Attraction: The Basics of the Teaching of Abraham*. Carlsbad, CA: Hay House, Inc., 2006.

HILL, NAPOLEON. *Think and Grow Rich*. Renaissance Books, 2001.

HILL NAPOLEON and W. CLEMENT STONE. *Success Through a Positive Mental Attitude*. New York, NY: Pocket Books, 1977.

HOLLIWELL, RAYMOND. *Working with the Law*. Camarillo, CA: DeVorss and Company, 2005.

HOLMES, ERNEST. *Basic Ideas of Science of Mind.* Camarillo, CA: DeVorss and Company, 1957.

JAMPOLSKY, GERALD G. *Love Is Letting Go of Fear.* Toronto, Canada: Bantam Books, 1970.

KEYES, KEN, JR. *Handbook to Higher Consciousness.* Marina del Ray, CA: Living Love Publications, DeVorss and Company, 1972.

KEYES, KEN, JR. *Prescriptions for Happiness.* Marina del Ray, CA: Living Love Publications, DeVorss and Company.

KEYES, KEN, JR. *Taming Your Mind.* St. Mary, KY: Living Love Publications, 1975.

KOHN, ALFIE. *Unconditional Parenting: Moving from Rewards and Punishments to Love and Reason.* New York, NY: Atria Books, 2005.

LEBOEUF, MICHAEL, *Imagineering: How to Profit from Your Creative Powers,* New York, NY: McGraw-Hill Book Co., 1980.

LOSIER, MICHAEL J. *Law of Attraction: The Science of Attracting More of What You Want and Less of What You Don't.* New York, NY: Hachette Book Group USA, 2003.

MACLEOD, WILLIAM M. and GAEL S. MACLEOD. *Mind over Weight.* Englewood Cliffs, NJ: Prentice-Hall, Inc., 1981.

MALTZ, MAXWELL. *Psychocybernetics.* New York, NY: Pocket Books, 1960.

MCKAY, MATTHEW, MARTHA DAVIS and PATRICK FANING. *Thoughts and Feelings: The Art of Cognitive Stress Intervention.* Richmond, CA: New Harbinger, 1981.

MOORMAN, CHICK. *Parent Talk: How to Talk to Your Children in Language That Builds Self-Esteem and Encourages Responsibility.* Merrill, MI: Personal Power Press, 1998.

MOORMAN, CHICK. *Spirit Whisperers: Teachers Who Nourish a Child's Spirit.* Merrill, MI: Personal Power Press, 2001.

MOORMAN, CHICK. *Talk Sense to Yourself: The Language of Personal Power.* Merrill, MI: Personal Power Press, 1985.

MOORMAN, CHICK and NANCY WEBER. *Teacher Talk: What It Really Means.* Merrill, MI: Personal Power Press, 1989.

MOORMAN, CHICK and THOMAS HALLER. *Couple Talk: How to Talk Your Way to a Great Relationship.* Merrill, MI: Personal Power Press, 2003.

MOORMAN, CHICK and THOMAS HALLER. *The 10 Commitments: Parenting with Purpose.* Merrill, MI: Personal Power Press, 2005.

MOORMAN, CHICK and THOMAS HALLER. *The Only Three Discipline Strategies You Will Ever Need: Essential Tools for Busy Parents.* Merrill, MI: Personal Power Press, 2007.

MURPHY, JOSEPH. *Power of the Subconscious.* New

York, NY: Prentice-Hall, Inc., 1974.

MURPHY, JOSEPH. *The Cosmic Power Within You.* West Nyack, NY: Parker Publishing Co., Inc., 1968.

MURPHY, JOSEPH. *Your Infinite Power to Be Rich.* West Nyack, NY: Parker Publishing Co., Inc. 1966.

PAGE, GARY SCREATON. *Being the Parent You Want to Be: 12 Communication Skills for Effective Parenting.* Nevada City, CA: Performance Learning Systems, 1999.

PEALE, NORMAN VINCENT. *Positive Imaging: The Powerful Way to Change Your Life.* Tappon, NJ: Fleming H. Revell Co., 1982.

PONDER, CATHERINE. *Dynamic Law of Prosperity.* Camarillo, CA: DeVorss and Company, 1985.

ROSS, RUTH. *Prospering Woman.* Mill Valley, CA: Whatever Publishing Co., 1982.

SHINN, FLORENCE SCOVEL. *The Game of Life and How to Play It.* Marina del Ray, CA: DeVorss and Co., 1925.

TEUTSCH, JOEL MORIE and CHAMPION K. TEUTSCH. *From Here to Greater Happiness or How to Change Your Life for Good.* Los Angeles, CA: Price/Stern/Sloan Publishers, Inc., 1959.

TRACY, BRIAN. *Universal Law of Success and Achievement.* Nightingale-Conant Corporation, 1991.

WATTLES, WALLACE. *The Science of Getting Rich.* Top of the Mountain Publishing, 1910.

OUR VISION:
HEALING ACRES

A portion of the proceeds from all of our books is used to maintain an equine retirement ranch. One dollar from each book sold will go toward the support of **Healing Acres Equine Retirement Ranch.**

The goal of Healing Acres Ranch is to provide a peaceful and caring environment for aged horses that have devoted many years of service. It will include a low-stress atmosphere, room to exercise and graze freely, adequate shelter, and preventive and attentive health care for all horses.

Other services planned for Healing Acres Ranch include therapeutic riding for persons with disabilities and equine-assisted psychotherapy.

If you wish to make a donation beyond the purchase of this book, please contact Thomas or Chick at the Healing Minds Institute via e-mail at **thomas@thomashaller.com.**

Thank you for helping us support this important vision.

O T H E R B O O K S
A N D P R O D U C T S
www.personalpowerpress.com

For Parents

THE ONLY THREE DISCIPLINE STRATEGIES YOU WILL EVER NEED: Essential Tools for Busy Parents, by Chick Moorman and Thomas Haller ($14.95)

THE 10 COMMITMENTS: Parenting with Purpose, by Chick Moorman and Thomas Haller ($19.95)

PARENT TALK: How to Talk to Your Children in Language That Builds Self-Esteem and Encourages Responsibility, by Chick Moorman ($14.00)

THE PARENT ADVISOR: 60 Articles to Ease Your Parenting Concerns, CD by Chick Moorman and Thomas Haller ($19.95)

THE LANGUAGE OF RESPONSE-ABLE PARENTING, 5-CD set featuring Chick Moorman ($39.95)

THE PARENT TALK SYSTEM: The Language of Response-Able Parenting, Facilitator's Manual, by Chick Moorman, Sarah Knapp, and Judith Minton ($300.00)

PARENT TALK FOCUS CARDS, by Chick Moorman ($10.00)

WINNING THE WHINING WARS, DVD by Thomas Haller ($19.95)

INSPIRING CHILDREN TO WRITE, DVD by Thomas Haller and Reese Haller ($19.95)

WHERE THE HEART IS: Stories of Home and Family, by Chick Moorman ($14.95)

For Educators

SPIRIT WHISPERERS: Teachers Who Nourish a Child's Spirit, by Chick Moorman ($24.95)

TEACHER TALK: What It Really Means, by Chick Moorman and Nancy Weber ($14.95)

OUR CLASSROOM: We Can Learn Together, by Chick Moorman and Dee Dishon ($19.95)

Miscellaneous

COUPLE TALK: How to Talk Your Way to a Great Relationship, by Chick Moorman and Thomas Haller ($24.95)

DENTAL TALK: How to Manage Children's Behavior with

Effective Verbal Skills, by Thomas Haller and Chick Moorman ($24.95)

TALK SENSE TO YOURSELF: The Language of Personal Power, by Chick Moorman ($14.95)

www.personalpowerpress.com
(877) 360-1477
P.O Box 547
Merrill, MI 48637